9780068576691U

PSYCHOLOGICAL BACKGROUNDS OF ADULT EDUCATION

*Papers Presented at a Syracuse University Conference
October, 1962, Sagamore, New York*

Edited by RAYMOND G. KUHLEN
Professor of Psychology, Syracuse University

CENTER *for the* **STUDY OF LIBERAL EDUCATION FOR ADULTS**

THE CENTER *for the* **STUDY OF LIBERAL EDUCATION FOR ADULTS** was established in 1951 by a grant from the Fund for Adult Education to work with universities seeking to initiate or improve programs of liberal education for adults. The purpose of the Center is "to help American higher education develop greater effectiveness and a deeper sense of responsibility for the liberal education of adults." Communications may be addressed to the Director, 4819 Greenwood Avenue, Chicago 15, Illinois.

Copyright 1963 by the Center for the Study of Liberal Education for Adults. All rights reserved.

PRINTED IN U.S.A.

FOREWORD

This volume is a result of a conference titled "Psychological Backgrounds of Adult Education." The conference was attended by a group of leading adult educators who were invited to participate in a continuing education program.

The conference was held at the Sagamore Conference Center of Syracuse University. The broad purpose was to initiate a dialogue between administrators of adult education and psychologists. Hopefully, this dialogue would enable adult educators to become more effective in their efforts to conduct educational programs for adults, and also would help psychologists to focus more attention on kinds of questions that adult educators are asking. The conference was organized to facilitate the occurrence of this dialogue by having a psychologist, an educational psychologist, and an adult educator speak on major topics.

The format was to have this group of psychologists present, in their own terms, the latest research in their field which hopefully would have relevance to the field of adult education. In general, it was felt that it would be more appropriate for the psychologists to present the latest developments in the field without having to take the second step in determining the implications for the education of adults. Yet in reports of their research, the educational psychologist and the adult educator might find many generalizations for adult education. In this way, it was expected that the findings of research might become more readily useful to administrators of adult education.

Special thanks are due the several discussants who commented upon the main papers. It was originally intended to publish their comments along with the main papers, but this proved impractical. William A. Owens of Purdue University and Harry L. Miller of Hunter College served as discussants of Birren's paper. Robert Kleemeier of Washington University and Paul H. Sheats of the University of California (Los Angeles) discussed the paper by Neugarten. David P. Ausubel of the University of Illinois and Fr. Richard T. Deters of Xavier University (Cincinnati) discussed Kuhlen's paper. McKeachie's paper was discussed by Bettye M. Caldwell of Syracuse University and Earnest Brandenburg of Washington University. To these individuals goes much of the credit for bridging the gap between the formal papers which emphasized the technical literature and the applicational interests which characterized the participants in the conference. To them also goes much of the credit for sparking the discussions and making the conference itself a successful endeavor.

An additional purpose of the dialogue was to encourage research in a basic field such as psychology. If research workers had further understanding of adult education, including practical problems, they might pursue additional research projects of relevance to adult education. Likewise adult educators who are conversant with latest research might make more pertinent suggestions for research projects.

The contents of this volume are intended to help adult educators to: increase their knowledge of the contributions of psychology to the field of adult education; develop an interest in discussing these ideas with their colleagues; and perform, or encourage, further research on topics of special interest.

At the present time, a conference similar to this one in psychology is being planned on the subject of "Sociological Backgrounds of Adult Education." Future conferences are also being considered which would deal with philosophy and with interdisciplinary approaches to the problems of adult educators.

The idea for the conference which led to this publication was first advanced by James B. Whipple, Assistant Director, Center for the Study of Liberal Education for Adults. The editor of this volume is Raymond Kuhlen, Professor of Psychology, Syracuse University, who also served as academic chairman of the conference. Both of these gentlemen merit a special note of appreciation. Clifford L. Winters, Jr., Roy Ingham, and Robert Snow, all of University College, served as the remaining members of the committee which made the conference a successful educational venture.

The Center for the Study of Liberal Education for Adults provided some initial support for the conference and has assumed the expense of publication.

July, 1963

Alexander N. Charters
Dean, University College,
Syracuse University

TABLE OF CONTENTS

	Page
Foreword	v
I. Psychology and Adult Education: Introductory Comments by Raymond G. Kuhlen	1
II. Adult Capacities To Learn by James E. Birren	8
III. Personality Changes During the Adult Years by Bernice L. Neugarten	43
IV. Motivational Changes During the Adult Years by Raymond G. Kuhlen	77
V. Psychological Characteristics of Adults and Instructional Methods in Adult Education by W. J. McKeachie	114
List of Participants	148

I

PSYCHOLOGY AND ADULT EDUCATION: INTRODUCTORY COMMENTS

Raymond G. Kuhlen
Syracuse University

The psychology which underlies an effective adult education program is not dissimilar to that which underlies education at any level. Basically, this consists of the psychology of the learner—his capacities, his motivations, his personality—and the psychology of the learning and instructional process. The psychology of adult education differs from the psychology of elementary and secondary education not so much in its principles as in the descriptive data which specify ways in which adults differ among themselves and from students typically found in elementary and secondary schools.

For practical if not theoretical reasons, the adult educator must be psychologically more sophisticated and sensitive than his elementary, secondary, or collegiate level counterpart. Adults are present in adult programs because of their own choosing and are likely to remain there only insofar as what is offered and instructional procedures employed are related to his needs, wants, and capacities. This is not to say that the educator in the elementary or secondary level should employ a less adequate "psychology," but rather that he can "get away with" ineptness with less danger of losing his audience. The adult educator must be much more sensitive to the psychological character of his clientele not only in his efforts to construct an image of adult education as an important resource for meeting the needs of adult living, a matter of substantial importance in affecting initial contact with students, but also in constructing a useful curriculum and devising effective instructional methodologies for those who do enroll.

The Purposes of the Conference—and This Monograph

Although the preceding paragraph has tended to emphasize the practical importance of an adequate "psychology of adult education," the materials presented in this volume are not presented with a view to immediate and direct application. The conference at which these papers were presented, and consequently this volume itself, was designed to provide the opportunity for a dialogue between leaders in the field of adult education and psychologists who have concerned themselves with the study of changes that occur as a person negotiates the adult life span from the 20's onward. It is hoped that the present "dialogue" may represent the beginning of other conversations between adult educators and social scientists[1] which may have the long-term effect not only of influencing practice but also of shaping the character of the research undertaken by psychologists interested in adult education.

Presented in this volume are four main papers summarizing the research dealing with (a) adult capacities to learn, (b) changing personality during the adult years, (c) changing motivation, with these topics brought to a focus in the final paper on (d) instructional methods in adult education as related to the personal characteristics of adults. Although many other topics might have been included, those selected seemed most important for consideration within the time available. The presentation of these papers in the present form will serve to make available in a single source summaries of much of the psychological literature relevant to adult education.

The contributors of the major papers were invited to address themselves to basic considerations rather than to applications. Although only the major papers are presented in this publication, at the conference itself each paper was followed by comments by two discussants, each of whom was asked to make appropriate translations and applications of the information presented in the major papers to adult education, to suggest direction in which psychological research might move in order to facilitate the best development of adult education, and where appropriate, to criticize the papers and make additions.[2] It was hoped that the comments

---

1. Syracuse University is planning a second conference on "Sociological Backgrounds of Adult Education" under the chairmanship of Dr. Hobert Burns, to be held in October, 1963.

2. As noted in the foreword to this monograph, it was originally planned to include the discussants' comments in this publication. Although this did not prove feasible, the editor wishes to record his personal appreciation of their contributions. Their names are recorded in the foreword.

of the discussants, one of whom was a psychologist interested in application, the other an adult educator, would at least serve to stake out the beginnings of a bridge between the developing science of the psychology of adult life and its application in a field which may well prove to be the major frontier of modern educational efforts.

Age as a Variable

As the reader encounters material presented in subsequent chapters he will become quickly aware that most of the facts are ordered in terms of the ages of the adults studied. Why this focus upon age? Although many stereotypes related to adult education ("You can't teach an old dog new tricks") involve assumptions regarding age differences, it is readily evident that age in and of itself is of little theoretical significance or practical importance in a naturalistic learning situation. But whether we like it or not, age is one of the key items of descriptive information we record about people, and a peg on which many misconceptions, as well as sound common-sense generalizations, are hung. It thus becomes an important task to explore the age relatedness of the factors basic to education, which do change with age. Age is time—time in which other things of psychological importance happen; time during which habits of study get rusty, previous knowledge is forgotten, roles change, energy level shifts, and demands and goals become different. The latter variables are factors of tremendous significance not only in determining the nature of the curriculum or program but also in determining reaction to educational methodologies.

Even though, as subsequent chapters will show, substantial age trends occur during the adult years, it is highly probable that the selection processes which operate in determining the nature of the student body with whom adult educators deal, especially in the university context, will markedly reduce the range of differences due to age. In the main, adult education attracts young adults, those who are caught up in the problems of career development and family rearing, and who see adult education as a means of implementing progress in these areas. However, there are some indications that this picture is changing rapidly. Technological developments have caused adult education programs to get involved in the professional refurbishing of adults of all ages. And displacement of workers by automation is forcing middle aged and older adults of non-professional skills into non-university retraining programs. Thus, it is probable that although selective factors have operated in the past to markedly reduce age as an important factor in adult education, it is unlikely that this circumstance will long continue to the same degree.

It is improbable, on the other hand, that such "enforced" return to school on the part of oldsters will be spontaneous in the liberal arts field. It might be anticipated that those concerned with the liberal education of adults, as are university orientated programs, will find that efforts to broaden the scope of this phase of adult education will be successful to the degree that differences associated with age are seen as important. Apparently it now attracts young adults more so than middle age or older adults, presumably because of lack of concern for, or lack of understanding of, the character of the older adult and the ways in which adult education programs might serve his particular needs.

Individual Differences vs. Mean Trends

There is a strong tendency for psychologists and other social scientists—as well as educators—to focus upon central tendencies when describing and comparing different groups. Differences between means of groups are typically presented in research reports and textbooks. Often little emphasis is placed upon the broad range of individual differences that may characterize these groups. In the case of developmental studies of adult life, age trends may be hardly discernible through direct inspection of the data. They become evident only when "summarized out" by the computation and plotting of means. Pressures of journal space, the use of high speed computers, and conventions regarding choice of statistical techniques have all conspired to make reporting of detailed distributions of data unfashionable or inconvenient. It is thus necessary to draw upon an investigation of a generation ago to illustrate this point as has been done in Table 1. Here are the scores on the Army Alpha Intelligence Tests from the well-known Jones and Conrad study published in 1933. Although asterisks have been inserted to mark the mean for each age group, the remarkable characteristic of this table is the range of individual differences.

Although age is one of the many factors influencing individual variations among adults, it may well be among the least important, at least over a broad age range of adult years. It is probable that from the viewpoint of the adult educator, differences due to such factors (and their

Table 1

Army Alpha Intelligence Test Scores of 1191 Individuals in Age from 10 to 60 in Certain New England Communities. The mean for each age group is indicated by an asterisk.

Score	10	11	12	13	14	15	16	17	18	19-21	22-24	25-29	30-34	35-39	40-44	45-49	50-54	55-59
200										2		1	1					1
190								1	1		1	1		1	4		1	
180		2		1	2	1	1		2	2			3	3	3	2	2	1
170			2	2	1		5		2	6	1	2	2	—	4	1	2	2
160		2	1	4	4	2	4	4	2	2	3	2	2	1	6	5	1	1
150			2	3	4	4	6	3	1	4		4	5	4	7	3	2	1
140		11	8	7	5	3	6	1	3	5	3	4	9	7	5	1	7	
130		11	7	9	13	2	8	6	1	1	4	1	7	8	6	5	3	1
120		3*	5	6*	1*	6	3	1	6	6	4		7	6	6	3	3	1
110	8*	8	10*	14	9	9	5*	4*	5*	3*	3*	8	5	5	5*	3	3*	2
100	4	11	9	5	7	8*	10	7	3	9	3*	6	2	7	9*	7*	2*	5*
90	7	11	16	6	4	8	5	3	3	5	2	12*	11*	11*	10	5	4	2
80	2	1	4	5	3	6	5	4	3	10	6	10	12	5	5	8	5	5
70	7	1	1	6	3	3	5	4	8	7	3	12	8	5	7	11	6	2
60	2	1	1	5	3	3	5	2	1	11	2	6	8	9	8	3	7	2
50	2	4	1		2	2	4	4	5	1	4	9	8	6	5	4	3	6
40						1	3		1	6	3	3	7	8	3	2	3	
30					1	1			1	1	1	3	6	7	3	4	2	6
20						1	1				1	1	5	3	6			1
10			1		1		1					2	5	—	1		2	
0-9												1	1					1
Total	34	55	65	71	56	61	75	50	46	87	44	88	106	96	97	68	59	33
Mean	44	47	57	60	76	86	93	97	97	101	92	90	87	85	92	81	81	70

Source: H. E. Jones and H. S. Conrad, The Growth and Decline of Intelligence, A Study of a Homogeneous Group Between the Ages of Ten and Sixty. Genetic Psychology Monographs, 1933, 15, 223-98.

correlates) as sex, social status, educational and occupational level, and marital status are those that have greatest relevance. However, a major task of future research is the ordering of these variables in terms of their importance in the adult education situation. To the degree that these factors and their personality and ability correlates turn out to be age related, age assumes greater importance as a meaningful index in adult education.

Single Dimensions of Adult Personality versus Their Interaction in the Educational Process

Modern research in educational psychology has made clear that an understanding of the learning process will be achieved largely to the degree to which we investigate and grasp the significance of the <u>interactions</u> among various dimensions of individual personality, curriculum, personalities of instructors and co-learners, and the instructional methodologies employed. Although McKeachie has done a superlative job of bringing these variables together in the final chapter of this volume, it seems desirable to call attention to the importance of such interaction at the outset. Although psychologically "everything happens at once," convenience of exposition requires that attention be directed to one variable at a time. The writer of each chapter has focused upon the variable assigned to him and has emphasized that variable to the neglect of others. This does not mean that he is unaware, nor should the reader be unaware, of the importance of the interaction among these and other variables. While it is possible at the present stage of our knowledge to show the relationship of age to some of the more important variables taken one at a time, available evidence does <u>not</u> permit an empirical description of how these interactions change with age. It was thus necessary for McKeachie to neglect the age variable in order to emphasize the interaction of other factors in the learning situation. It is not improbable that certain variables may be more important in this interaction at one age than at another. But the unraveling of such complexities must necessarily await more adequate theorizing and empirical investigations than presently have been accomplished.

A Methodological Caution

The fact that the focus of much of this volume is upon adult age trends in abilities, personality, and motivation, requires a caution that may not have occurred to readers who have previously given little attention to the matter of data on adult life and aging. This caution relates to the difference between cross-sectional and longitudinal studies. By and large, psychologists have tended to favor the longitudinal study, primarily because it permits an analysis of <u>changes</u> that occur with age, an analysis of individual patterns of aging and the factors related thereto, and the comparison of individuals at different points in their lives. These are obviously important matters, which can be investigated only by studying the same individuals over time.

In contrast, the cross-sectional methodology has been employed largely as a matter of convenience because of its practical advantages. Data can be collected more efficiently with less expenditure of time and money and findings can be made available in relatively short time. As a consequence, most of the available information on the adult years is the result of cross-sectional investigations. To draw inferences regarding the nature of age <u>changes</u> from cross-sectional data, as a developmental psychologist must, involves certain risks and important dangers of error. While profiting from the understandings such studies yield, the adult educator must also concern himself to a substantial degree with age differences. While technical criticism of cross-sectional investigation is not to be ignored, it is of less importance when concern is with the <u>current</u> differences among class members. In many instances, such differences represent the relevant differences for method and program. On the other hand, when the adult educator concerns himself with how students become the way they are or with evaluation of the outcomes of adult education (when he follows up a group of students over time and compares them with appropriate control groups), he has shifted from a concern with cross-sectional differences to longitudinal changes. Although some sensitivity to methodological issues is thus necessary to an understanding of data on adult years, it is fortunate that for many purposes cross-sectional studies yield exactly the kind of information with which the adult educator must be primarily concerned.

II

ADULT CAPACITIES TO LEARN

James E. Birren
National Institute of Mental Health

There is a natural human interest element in whether our capacity to learn over the adult years constricts or, barring ill health, continues to expand. While proverbs and anecdotes might satisfy the casually interested person, the educator and the psychologist must turn to a body of technical information to form their opinions about the changes in adult capacities to learn. It is of interest that when Thorndike published his book in 1928 on adult learning he compared two age groups, 20-24 and 35 years or more. The latter group had an average age of 42 years. A contemporary study of aging would hardly regard a group with an average age of 42 as old and indeed the dialogue concerning aging and capacity to learn has tended to be shifted to comparisons of adults over 65 with those in their twenties. With the gradual rise in years of educational attainment more adults are aging with a positive attitude toward abstract learning as well as learning of psychomotor skills. One example in recent years of the expectancy of adult capacity for learning was shown by the FAA decision to permit commercial airline pilots to train to shift from flying piston airplanes to jet planes up to the age of 55. The idea of an individual learning to fly such a dramatically new type of plane at the age of 50 would come as quite a shock to students of learning in the days of Thorndike.

Definitions

In order to discuss the relations of adult age to learning, certain definitions and distinctions are useful. Learning may be defined as a relative lasting modification of behavior as a result of experience. To be regarded as learned, the "experience" must be registered, retained, and recalled. It is only by testing or examining for the effects of the experience some time later that one may judge whether learning has taken place. Intuition suggests that what we are getting at in discussions of learning is a matter of sheer plasticity of behavior. Without evidence from the neurophysiologists of what this ultimate plasticity of behavior consists, our descriptions of learning cannot be reduced to an ultimate physical or chemical state. There is little reason to doubt, however, that a physical or chemical modification will eventually be found corresponding to the registration and retention of an experienced event.

In his discussion of theories of learning in relation to aging, Kay (1959) quoted James' discussion of plasticity as "possession of a structure weak enough to yield to an influence but strong enough not to yield all at once." Particularly, in relation to aging, we might with profit emphasize this balance between plasticity and permanency of behavior for if the nervous system is excessively plastic in response to experience much of what we regard as important would be transient in its influence. In the definition of learning as a relatively permanent modification of behavior the term <u>relative</u> implies for the individual the advantage of adaptive behavior while retaining the advantages of stability. While the teacher of formal subject matters, such as mathematics and foreign languages, may regret the shifting impermanency of the day's classroom results, the psychotherapist treating an adult may regret the permanency of certain undesirable behavior. It may be too much to expect to have our "toast buttered on both sides," by having those learned aspects of behavior we regard as advantageous very enduring, and those elements of behavior we consider undesirable highly plastic. Since the older adult has already acquired his social skills and other processes we would regard as elementary, such as, language and arithmetic computation, we tend to be more interested in specific aspects of learning, or rather the adult capacities to modify certain areas of behavior, rather than his overall plasticity as we are with a child who has "the whole row to hoe."

Modifying Conditions

Many conditions will affect overall learning performance which we would not regard as part of the primary learning process. One of these is motivation which influences the intensity or frequency of the individual in exposing himself to the learning experience. In studies of animal learning it is common practice to deprive the animals of food for a short length of time so that they will move toward appropriate discriminations to get food as a reward. Food deprivation is therefore regarded as a way of motivating animals to learn. In older animals, however, it is known that the amount of food deprivation equal to the deprivation of young will produce less in the way of motivation. Clearly one must be able to manipulate conditions of motivation independent of age and the type of material to be learned if one is to decide upon the importance of particular variables. Endocrine changes of aging very likely alter drive levels or motivation which enter into the learning situation. Yet another example is speed of performance which may limit the amount of exposure the older organism may have to the learning situation. A slow human or animal can stretch out the sequence of elements in a learning task, which may seriously interfere with acquisition since temporal contiguity is an important aspect of learning.

While changes in physiological drive states, speed, and perceptual acuity may limit the older individual's learning performance other factors may facilitate it. Novelty of a learning situation may operate in favor of the older person's learning. While it is often thought that a learning situation for an aged adult is more threatening than the same situation for a young adult in school, it is also true that the learning situation is in itself sufficiently novel to intrigue and capture the interest of the older adult. There remains much to be done in studies of the relative contributions of secondary factors in adult learning so that the learning of older adults can be maximized by proper control.

Age, Industrial Change, and Retraining

Since adults are less frequently than children in learning situations where individual records of progress are kept, our picture of adult learning is not nearly as complete or organized as is that for children and young adults. This situation is changing as psychomotor skills are increasingly taken over by machines. Whereas previous generations could view children as learners and adults as doers we now find that machines are taking over man's tasks at an uncomfortably fast rate and adults are returned to the role of learner, a rather pleasant prospect if we regard a lifetime of learning as a most edifying human form of existence. Continuing adult learning can no longer be looked upon as an oddity but rather as an increasingly common feature of life in a complex society.

An example of the extent of industrial change and its impact on adult learning requirements is provided by a study of worker retraining by the

Department of Labor (1963). Although a pilot study it does serve to outline some of the issues which will be faced with greater frequency. Four companies were studied in which recent technological changes have required retraining of employees. The study had to be limited to those companies which maintained systematic personnel records. It is of interest that the four companies were the only ones in about 100 canvassed which kept records of individual performance during retraining, had workers over and under 40 years, and had data on educational level. Over two thousand workers were covered in different occupations: oil refinery production workers, airline maintenance mechanics, engineers, aircraft factory technicians and craftsmen, and telephone company operators.

The industrial changes were those primarily resulting from automation. It would seem that there is a somewhat different cognitive load placed on the worker in an automated plant. He returns to an almost classroom-like learning situation in some instances for extensive preparation or retraining. For example, a petroleum company changed dramatically from a previous step-at-a-time process to a "straight through" method of production. In the new system the whole plant worked as one unit or not at all: no part could stop for 12 hours without the whole plant stopping. This required the operators to depend upon a highly instrumental control system and to have knowledge about processes in all parts of the plant. One senses that the worker's skill changes from a limited operation in time and place to an anticipatory function. Speed, strength, and dexterity thus become less important than long term integration of abstract information and planning of strategy.

In preparing for the petroleum plant change over, the company gave a series of courses of instruction to 82 operating workers and 18 instrumentation workers. For the operators, two sets of courses were given, each 8 hours a day, 5 days a week. One course went for a total of 120 hours and another for 160 hours. A third set of courses was given 4 to 8 hours a week over a two-week period.

For the instrument workers one set of courses was arranged by company staff and the other by a local university staff. The content ranged from elementary physics through electronics and construction and maintenance of specific instruments.

Table 1 gives the results of the production worker training in relation to worker age. Each trainee was compared in grade with the median group performance and comparisons are made between the proportion of young and older workers above and below the median. Using this method of analysis the age differences are not impressive; they further become minimized if workers with the same level of education are compared (Table 2). The older instrument workers were if anything somewhat better than the young (under 40) in the training courses (Table 3).

The results from the aircraft plant and from the airline maintenance employees might be examined but the data on retraining of long distance telephone operators provides a more interesting contrast. The new task of the operators involved the substitution of an IBM card for a previous paper form. The changes were more in the nature of a shift in a well established psychomotor skill, than of a more fundamental change, as in the petroleum workers task. Rather than writing numbers on slips of paper, the operator was required to read down and mark small spaces in vertical columns which correspond to numbers. To process the card accurately in the computer at the next stage, the marking must be done accurately: marking errors result in billing errors. The operator must also do the marking rapidly. To establish the new pattern each operator was given a two-day period of retraining involving both marking and reading of cards. The trainees were called on standard telephone apparatus, as in an actual working situation, and the trainee was required to record and place the call in the new standard manner. The second phase involved the use of the marked IBM cards in placing calls. Trainees were required to place calls which had been recorded on a deck of 30 cards; both speed and accuracy were emphasized.

Performance was described by five measures: total number of tickets marked, total number of errors, total number of items omitted, number of omissions per card, and the difference between the total tickets marked and the sum of errors and omissions. Table 4 shows that the proportion of trainees with above average scores declined with increasing age on 4 of the 5 measures: errors tended not to be different with age.

When differences in educational level are adjusted, the age differences in performance were reduced (Tables 5 and 6). When the results of interpretation of tickets are examined with respect to speed and errors, trainees over 45 did not do as well as the younger group. The authors observed, "It is noteworthy, however, that the performance record of older trainees,

Table 1

Production Workers at Oil Refinery: Level of Performance
of Younger and Older Trainees on Training Courses

Name and Duration of Course	Younger Trainees			Older Trainees[1]		
	Number of Trainees	Per Cent Above Average Grade	Per Cent Below Average Grade	Number of Trainees	Per Cent Above Average Grade	Per Cent Below Average Grade
1. Zone A (3 weeks)	12	58	42	10	40	60
2. Zone B-D (3 weeks)	10	50	50	11	45	55
3. Zone C (3 weeks)	10	60	40	11	36	64
4. Zone D (3 weeks)	5	80	20	5	20	80
5. Zone A (4 weeks)	15	47	53	15	53	47
6. Zone B (4 weeks)	12	58	42	13	46	54
7. Zone C (4 weeks)	15	53	47	13	31	69
8. Zone D (4 weeks)	4	50	50	3	33	67
9. Zone A (2 years)	10	50	50	10	40	60
10. Zone B (2 years)	7	75	25	8	50	50
11. Zone C (2 years)	8	63	37	8	50	50
12. Zone D (2 years)	5	60	40	6	33	67

[1] Because of the small number of trainees in each course, it was necessary to use a different age criterion for each course. In Course 1 and 2, older trainees included those 47 years and over; Courses 3, 5 and 12, 43 years and over; Course 4, 51 years and over; Course 6, 52 years and over; Course 7, 49 years and over; Course 8, 48 years and over; Courses 9 and 11, 39 years and over; Course 10, 42 years and over.

Source (Tables 1 through 7): U.S. Department of Labor, Industrial Retaining Program for Technological Change—A Study of the Performances of Older Workers, Government Printing Office Bulletin 1368, 1963.

Table 2

Production Workers at Oil Refinery. Level of Performance of Older and Younger Trainees when Differences in Education Are Taken into Account.

Name and Duration of Course	Younger Trainees			Older Trainees[1]		
	Number of Trainees	Per Cent		Number of Trainees	Per Cent	
		Above Average Grade	Below Average Grade		Above Average Grade	Below Average Grade
1. Zone A (3 weeks)	12	50	50	9	45	55
2. Zone B-D (3 weeks)	10	40	60	9	67	33
3. Zone C (3 weeks)	10	50	50	10	50	50
4. Zone D (3 weeks)	3	33	67	4	50	50
5. Zone A (4 weeks)	12	58	42	13	46	54
6. Zone B (4 weeks)	12	67	33	10	40	60
7. Zone C (4 weeks)	11	82	18	13	31	69
8. Zone D (4 weeks)	5	40	60	2	100	0
9. Zone A (2 years)	12	58	42	6	33	66
10. Zone B (2 years)	6	50	50	4	50	50
11. Zone C (2 years)	8	50	50	8	63	37
12. Zone D (2 years)	4	25	75	4	75	25

[1] See footnote to Table 1.

Table 3

Instrument Mechanics at Oil Refinery. Per cent of Older and Younger Trainees who Received Grades Above and Below Average Test Scores.

| Name of Course | Younger Trainees ||| Older Trainees[1] |||
| | Number of Trainees | Per Cent || Number of Trainees | Per Cent ||
		Above Average Grade	Below Average Grade		Above Average Grade	Below Average Grade
1. Company course: Arithmetic	7	29	71	6	67	33
2. Company course: Fractions and decimals	8	47	53	7	71	29
3. Vendor course: Control valves	8	50	50	7	43	57
4. Vendor course: Controls and valves	8	50	50	6	67	33
5. Vendor course: Level indicators	8	50	50	6	50	50
6. University course: Generators and AC circuits	7	43	57	6	50	50

[1] Older trainees include those 40 years of age and over.

15

based on error using the old method of interpreting tickets, was about the same as the record for younger trainees. This suggests that, with further experiences using the new method, older trainees would probably achieve about the same level of performance as younger trainees."

Table 4

Telephone Operator Trainees: Level of Performance on Various Tests, by Age Group.

Test and Performance Level	Age Group (per cent)			
	18-24	25-34	35-44	45 and over
Number of Trainees	176	202	70	55
Number of tickets marked				
Above average[1]	54.0	51.5	41.4	25.5
Below average	46.0	48.5	58.6	74.5
Total number of errors				
Above average	43.7	49.5	58.6	52.7
Below average	56.3	50.5	41.4	47.3
Total number of omissions				
Above average	62.5	59.4	58.6	40.0
Below average	37.5	40.6	41.4	60.0
Ratio of omissions to tickets marked				
Above average	55.7	52.0	47.1	29.1
Below average	44.3	48.0	52.9	70.9
Marking efficiency index				
Above average	59.7	53.0	42.9	27.3
Below average	40.3	47.0	57.1	72.7

[1] Above average always indicates superior performances (e.g., more tickets, fewer errors).

This type of performance involving psychomotor coordination where speed is important has long been regarded as being especially difficult for older persons. One might express surprise that the age groups were not found to be even more different.

The authors of the report point out that this was a pilot study; many issues must be resolved before the results can be generalized to adult populations. So far as the main purposes of the study, however, the results do suggest that the chronological age of an adult is secondary to other identifiable individual characteristics that bear upon learning and occupational retraining. Although highly suggestive, the results should not be accepted as definitive regarding the relations of age and learning

Table 5

Telephone Operator Trainees. Level of Performance of Trainees with 8-11 Years of Education, on Various Tests, by Age Group.

| Test and Level of Performance | Age Group ||||
	18-24	25-34	35-44	45 and over
Number of trainees	<u>33</u>	<u>31</u>	<u>21</u>	<u>31</u>
	(Per Cent)			
Number of tickets marked Above average Below average	57.6 42.4	51.6 48.4	33.3 66.7	19.3 80.7
Total number of errors Above average Below average	45.4 54.6	64.5 35.5	61.9 38.1	38.7 61.3
Total number of omissions Above average Below average	63.6 36.4	77.4 22.6	61.9 38.1	45.2 54.8
Ratio of omissions to tickets marked Above average Below average	51.5 48.5	61.3 38.7	38.1 61.9	25.8 74.2
Marking efficiency index Above average Below average	60.6 39.4	67.7 32.3	47.6 52.4	22.6 77.4

capacity since the sample was small for particular age, education, and skill categories.

These examples of industrial studies of adult learning give a picture of the context within which contemporary adult learning may be done. The context of industrial learning seems to be moving toward that found in educational institutions. The distinction between real life learning and school learning seems to be breaking down. Perhaps the distinction between the laboratory and industrial learning situation is also less sharp than it was. However just as there are qualifications which must be introduced before laboratory studies of learning are generalized to daily life context, so results of industrial studies must be qualified before they are generalized to the population at large.

Industries select personnel upon entry and there is both voluntary and forced selection out over time. This means that workers in a particular industry over some arbitrary age, e.g., 45, are not representative

Table 6

Telephone Operator Trainees. Level of Performance in Marking Tickets of Trainees with 12 Years or More of Education, by Age Group.

Test and Level of Performance	Age Group			
	18-24	25-34	35-44	45 and over
Number of trainees	<u>142</u>	<u>158</u>	<u>44</u>	<u>18</u>
	(Per Cent)			

Number of tickets marked
  Above average
  Below average
	53.5
	46.5
		52.5
		47.5
			45.4
			54.6
				38.9
				61.1

Total number of errors
  Above average
  Below average
	43.7
	56.3
		48.7
		51.3
			63.6
			36.4
				77.8
				22.2

Total number of omissions
  Above average
  Below average
	62.7
	37.3
		56.3
		43.7
			54.6
			45.4
				27.8
				72.2

Ratio of omissions to tickets marked
  Above average
  Below average
	57.0
	43.0
		50.0
		50.0
			52.3
			47.7
				38.9
				61.1

Marking efficiency index
  Above average
  Below average
	59.9
	40.1
		50.0
		50.0
			40.9
			59.1
				38.9
				61.1

of the entrance age group or of the population at large. Furthermore, years of job experience make more probable interference or negative transfer effects to new job requirements. Laboratory experiments characteristically control for the level of initial experience so that age differences in rates of learning can be studied. Thus the laboratory deliberately studies a learning task whose content has never before been learned in order to minimize unequal positive or negative transfer. In industry, duration of experience varies with chronological age in a manner that is difficult to control.

The introduction of automated equipment into office procedures also has carried with it implications for adult learning. The Bureau of Labor (Bull. 1276, May, 1960) issued a report of a survey of this subject which

Table 7

Telephone Operator Trainees. Level of Performance on Tests Interpreting Tickets, by Age Group.

Tests and Level of Performance	Age Group			
	18-24	25-34	35-44	45 and over
Number of trainees	92	165	55	57
	(Per Cent)			
Speed using old method				
Above average	52.2	52.7	50.9	33.3
Below average	47.8	47.3	49.1	66.7
Errors using old method				
Above average	63.0	68.5	69.1	64.9
Below average	37.0	31.5	30.9	35.1
Speed using new method				
Above average	60.9	54.6	38.2	28.1
Below average	39.1	45.4	61.8	71.9
Errors using new method				
Above average	56.5	60.6	60.0	39.3
Below average	43.5	39.4	40.0	60.7
Speed difference				
Above average	55.4	54.6	49.1	31.8
Below average	44.6	45.4	50.9	68.2

indicates that persons selected for the newer programing and planning jobs tended to be men between the ages of 25 and 34 with some college education. While four out of five employees assigned to the new positions were upgraded, few women or older workers were chosen. While the job status of older workers was not much affected they tended not to be promoted to the newly created positions. Educational qualification was among the factors given for the lack of older worker promotion to the newer electronic positions. Presumably the lack of sufficient education on the part of older workers would preclude the mastery of the newer more abstract skills. Because of this supposition and the previous data showing differences in learning performance in relation to age and educational level it seems important to examine data on adult intelligence tests with regard to age and education.

Age and Performance on Intelligence Tests

Recent studies of mental test scores in relation to advancing age continue to show a differential pattern (see discussion by Jones, 1959). Some of the earlier differences of opinion about intelligence test scores and age are being resolved as results show that whether increments or decrements with age are obtained not only depend upon the nature of the sample populations used in cross sectional studies but also on the type of tests. In general, tests involving perceptual content show decrements with age whereas tests which allow for accumulated experience, e.g., vocabulary, show increments.

Bilash and Zubek (1962) found that perceptual and dexterity tests declined from the teens to the 70's whereas other tests, e.g., comprehension and verbal fluency, held up well until the mid-forties. Of interest are the correlations of their tests with education.

Table 8

Correlations of Mental Tests with Education from Bilash and Zubek (1962): Age Has Been Partialled Out.

Test	r
Memory	.20
Perception	.25
Dexterity	.29
Numerical	.37
Reasoning	.37
Comprehension	.37
Space	.40
Fluency	.42

These correlations with education are somewhat lower than those obtained if the negative correlation between age and education in the population is not controlled for, and may be compared with those of the WAIS obtained by Birren and Morrison (Table 9). Both the relation between age and test performance may be studied by removing the effects

Table 9

Wais Correlation Matrix: 11 Subtests and Age and Education.*

	1	2	3	4	5	6	7	8	9	10	11	12
1 Information	67											
2 Comprehension	62	54										
3 Arithmetic	66	60	51									
4 Similarities	47	39	51	41								
5 Digit Span	81	72	58	68	45							
6 Vocabulary	47	40	41	49	45	49						
7 Digit symbol	60	54	46	56	42	57	50					
8 Picture completion	49	45	48	50	39	46	50	61				
9 Block design	51	49	43	50	42	52	52	59	54			
10 Picture arrangement	41	38	37	41	31	40	46	51	59	46		
11 Object assembly	-07	-08	-08	-19	-19	-02	-46	-28	-32	-37	-28	
12 Age	66	52	49	55	43	62	57	48	44	49	40	-29
13 Education												

Note. N = 933 native-born white males and females, age range 25-64.
*Decimal points omitted.

21

of education; the relation of education and test performance may be studied by removing the effects of age. These points are illustrated in an analysis of the subtests of the Wechsler Adult Intelligence Scale (WAIS) in relation to age and education (Birren and Morrison, 1961).

A subset of the standardization data of the WAIS was drawn: results were based upon 933 subjects, native-born white, aged 25-64 years. All tests showed a significant correlation with years of education. In this age range, the correlation of test scores with years of education was greater than with chronological age. This may be seen graphically in Figure 1 which gives the mean curves by level of education. These data yield the important fact that in the age range of 25-64 years, individual differences in tests scores are more highly correlated with educational level than with chronological age. This result parallels that previously cited for the industrial studies wherein education level was significantly related to learning.

These findings do not imply that educational level was the cause of high test scores since initial mental ability influences the years of schooling. They also do not imply that there is no change with age in component mental abilities. In terms of relative variance it may be said that more variance is associated with level of education than with age. Age is significantly positive for a number of subtests, e.g., information and vocabulary, and significantly negative for, e.g., digit symbol and picture arrangement. Again this is not unlike the industrial learning studies in which the long distance telephone operators showed some decrement with age in a relatively high speed perceptual motor task, whereas in the other industrial learning tasks, which could be approached verbally in an unspeed context, showed little age difference. Obviously the pattern of mental abilities changes with age. This leads us to the issue of differential weighting of intelligence test results, e.g., should one give greater weight to the increments in scores or to the few tests showing decrements.
There is the question here of which items have greatest validity as indicators of adult mental capacity. In children this has been somewhat settled by adopting the criterion of school success. For children or young adults a valid intelligence test or item is one which bears a relationship to performance in mastering school subject matter. Lacking a similar obvious criterion, it is not possible to make decisions either about the appropriate content of adult intelligence tests or how to differentially

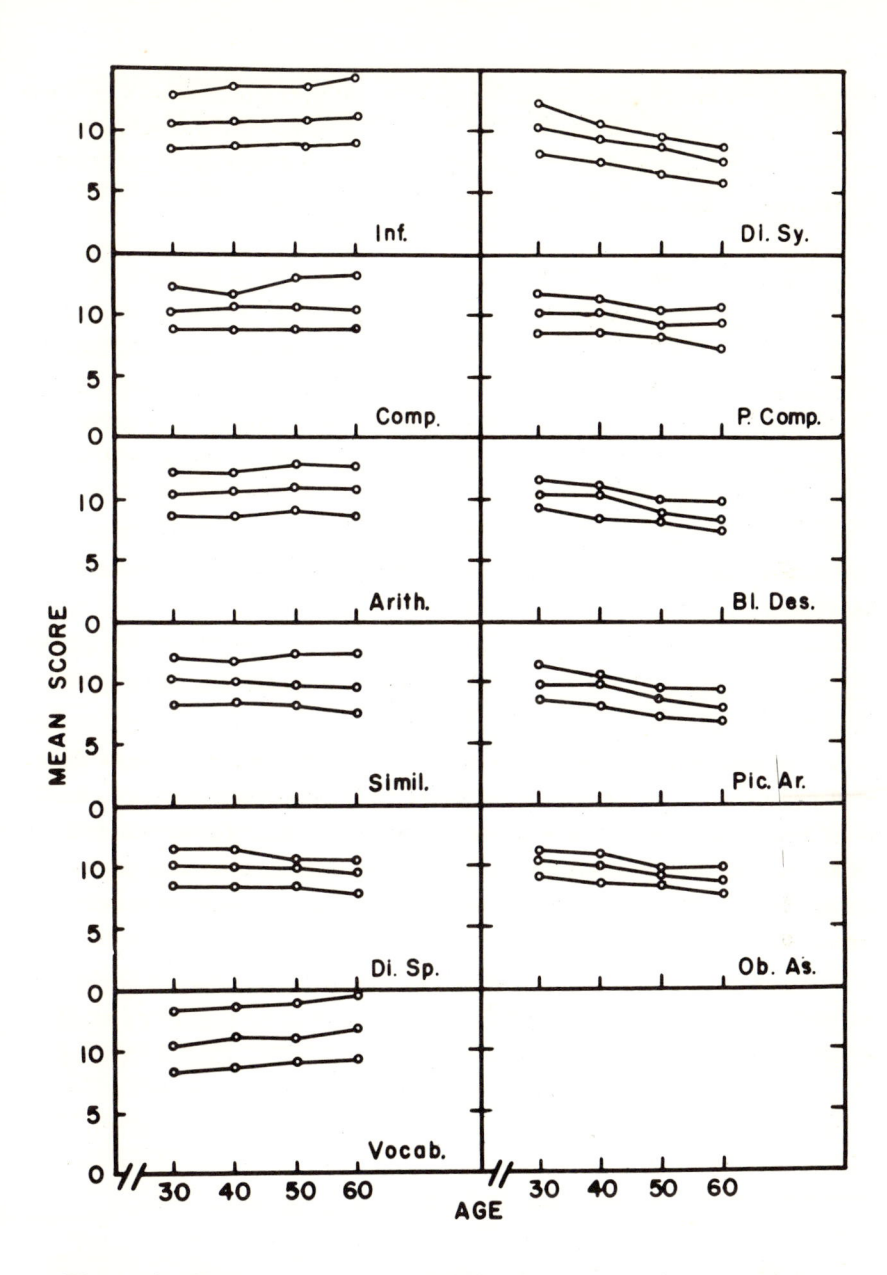

Figure 1. Mean scores on the WAIS subtests as a function of age and education. Upper curves for education 13 years and above; middle curves for 8-12 years; and lower curves for less than 8 years. Age intervals are 25-34, 35-44, 45-54, and 55-64 years (from Birren and Morrison, 1961).

weight types of items. The content of adult intelligence tests has been rightfully criticized as an unthoughtful borrowing from children's tests. Yet, until there is agreement upon what factor or group of factors can provide a criterion of adult intelligence there is little but intuition to guide efforts to select the content of adult tests.

The issue may be drawn even more specifically in the case of verbal tests which show a rise with age in a synonym test and a decline with age in a word selection test (Riegel, 1959). Whether there is some interference in the selection of a word when more are known with advancing age is not settled, but the point at issue is that of differential verbal performance measures. Is a synonym or word selection test a better measure of adult mental capacity? Obviously the matter of differential validity must be approached cautiously until the criterion problem is advanced.

The relevance of health to mental test performance is seen in the results of a study at the National Institute of Mental Health (Birren, et al., 1962). Figure 2 shows the mean WAIS subtest performance of two groups of socially competent elderly men, 27 men of good health, and 20 men with asymptomatic or subclinical disease.

The healthy subjects show a mean verbal performance higher than that expected for young adults but lower on tests already known to decline with age, e.g., the digit symbol test. The less healthy subjects are at the level of young subjects on the verbal tests and about the same as the other group on the age "sensitive" tests. One discerns here a differential effect of age and health.

Clark (1962) gave a group of 25 psychological and physiological tests to 102 males and females over the age range 20 to 70 years. He found a single large or general factor involving 19 of the 25 measures and accounting for almost all of the variance associated with age. He concluded, " . . . that, at the level of this analysis, aging occurs along a single dimension, measured best by blood pressure, lens accommodation and sound threshold, and less well by ability and speed tests." These results are important for they lend substance to the view that there is a common pattern of psychological changes associated with advancing age and having a normal psychophysiological basis rather than a pathogenetic basis.

A further differentiation of this concept was reported by Birren and Spieth (1962). While they found, as did Clark, a correlation of age with both psychomotor speed and blood pressure, their age-speed correlation

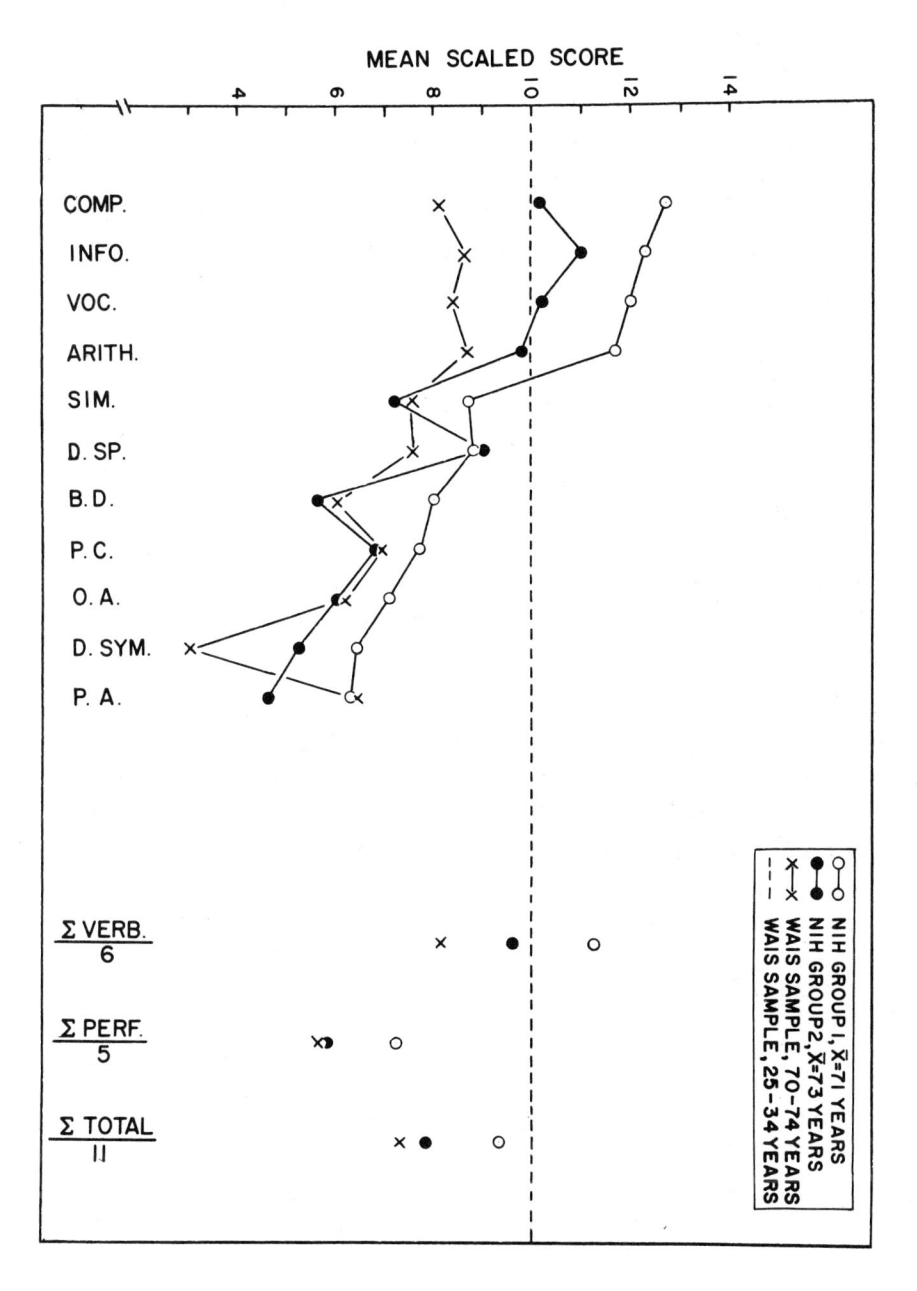

Figure 2. Mean performance on the WAIS subtests in relation to health and age. Adapted from Birren, Botwinick, Weiss, and Morrison (in press, 1962).

was higher than the age-blood pressure correlation. This led them to the view that the trend toward higher blood pressure with advancing age could not be regarded as the "cause" of slowing of psychomotor performance but possibly a reflection of a common change with advancing age in the regulation of the central nervous system of vegetative and behavioral functions. Patients with hypertension or coronary artery disease appear to show more marked psychomotor slowing than expected for age alone. The evidence again points to a separation of the effects of disease from a pattern of measurements representative of normal psychophysiological aging.

Twins over the age of 69 have been reported upon in an important series of papers. One of the basic findings is that the correlations between mental abilities of one-egg twins persists into the later years. Very significant for both the psychological and biological viewpoints was the fact that intra-pair differences in length of life remained smaller for one-egg twins than for two-egg twins (of the same sex) (Falek, Kallmann, Lorge, and Jarvik, 1960). It would appear that both longevity and mental abilities in later life are controlled or paced to some extent by hereditary factors.

In view of the fact that information items have generally been shown to increase with age, and perceptual and speed measures to decrease, there is interest in knowing which are more closely related to length of life. A ten year longitudinal study was carried out on 268 senescent twins, 48 were tested on three occasions (Jarvik, Kallmann, and Falek, 1962). A positive relationship was found between test scores and survival. It is of great interest that, "Comparison of mean scores of first, second, and third testings revealed statistically significant losses only on the two speeded performance tests (tapping and digit symbol). The decline trend on the other tests was less pronounced, although there was an interval of seven years between the second and third testing." The decline in tapping test speed over the three tests and the lower initial score of non-survivors clearly places the changes in psychomotor speed in the middle of an important matrix of relationships. The reported generality of the speed changes by Birren, Riegel, and Morrison (1962) indicates that they may not be regarded as non-cognitive, but rather imply changes in control over the use of stored information.

Longitudinal studies of mental abilities have given us more precise information about changes in individuals (Kleemeier, 1961; Jarvik, 1962; Owens, 1953; Bayley, 1955), though they have not resolved the problem of the criterion of adult intelligence. One which is suggested by the longitudinal studies is that of the prediction of survival. The use of such a criterion assumes that mental ability to some extent should parallel the remaining duration of life and as individuals approach the end of their lives, mental test scores should decline. There is actually some evidence for this in the studies of Kleemeier, and Jarvik. What is bothersome in this concept is the fact that the cause of death may influence the course of terminal decline with some individuals showing dramatic interruption of a full facultied existence while others undergo a protracted involution.

The longitudinal studies of mental abilities generally show significant decline for individuals beginning 70 years or later. From this one may suspect that if mental declines are sometimes seen in middle-aged adults, they are likely the result of diseases influencing the central nervous system rather than a part of a normal senescent program of aging. Cerebral arteriosclerosis, hypertension, and even coronary artery disease likely have cognitive and affective psychological concomitants (Spieth, 1962). Their effects and relationships should properly be distinguished from those age related behavioral characteristics which all members of the population eventually show.

Age, Brain Damage, and Mental Abilities

One commonly expressed opinion about the deficits in mental ability which appear in the mental test performance of some older individuals is that the deficit arises from brain damage. Mortality and verbal learning were shown to be related in psychiatric patients (N=30) by Sanderson and Inglis (1961). In selected patient populations they found a significant relationship between scores on verbal learning tests and mortality over a period less than two years. The obtained relationship between mental capacity and survival was greater between the psychological measurements and survival, than between survival and original diagnosis.

Reed and Reitan (1962) studied performance on a complex psychomotor task, among other reasons, " . . . to obtain additional evidence pertinent to the possibility that the normal aging process exerts an influence on performances in this kind of task situation similar to that of clinically established brain damage." In their study, 50 brain-damaged subjects were compared with 50 controls matched for age, education, sex, and race. The subjects were given three trials on the Seguin-Goddard form-board, and the data were analyzed with respect to levels of performance and improvement in relation to age and brain damage. Both age and brain damage proved to have a significant and marked influence on the absolute levels of performance but little on measurements of improvement over successive trials. Insofar as the task involves learning, the variables of age and brain damage did not affect ability to improve performance with practice.

In a study of the electroencephalogram in relation to mental functioning in older subjects leading normal lives, Obrist, et al. (1962) found little evidence of a relationship between the EEG and intelligence test performance. However, in subjects with medical and psychiatric disorders, low intelligence test scores were found to be associated with EEGs that deviated from young adult norms. They concluded, "The results suggest that age, per se, is not a crucial factor influencing the magnitude of EEG-intelligence test correlations. Rather it would appear that health status is the critical determinant of the degree of relationship." It should also be noted that correlations for individuals with arteriosclerosis were consistently higher than those without. These findings lead us to approach the older subject more individualistically and to expect that he will show mental test performance influenced by the absence or presence of forms of brain pathology more common in late life. Present evidence suggests that the effects of cerebral pathology are superimposed on or interacting with a pattern of change prototypic of normal aging.

Conditioning

One model of learning is that of classical conditioning; one type of conditioning used in relation to aging is the conditioned eye blink. Braun and Geiselhart (1959) conditioned the blink reflex to a light. In this case, a small illuminated patch was exposed in front of the subject for one second. After a half second a puff of air was directed at the cornea of the eye causing the subject to blink. In this pattern each subject was given 80 conditioning trials and 20 extinction trials during which the conditioned response could be expected to be modified. They compared the conditioning and extinction of the eye blink reflex in male subjects 8 to 10 years, 18 to 25 years, and 62 to 84 years. The results (Figure 3) showed a difference between the young subjects and the old subjects in the frequency of conditioned responses: older subjects proved to be relatively unconditionable. The authors favored the interpretation here that over many years of living that the eye blink becomes more adapted to environmental conditions and thus less susceptible to conditioning.

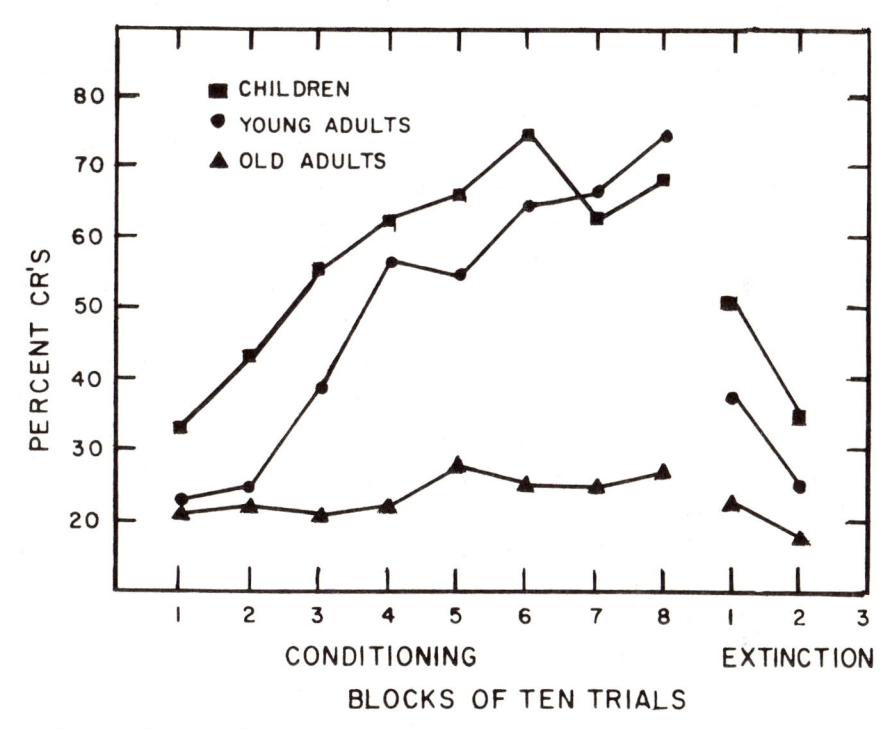

Figure 3. Per cent frequency of conditioned eyeblink responses on successive blocks of trials during conditioning and extinction for three age groups. Adapted from Braun and Geiselhart, 1959, by permission of the publisher, the American Psychological Association.

Conditioned hand withdrawal has also been studied in relation to age (Marinesco and Kreindler, 1934). In this study the unconditioned stimulus was an electric current which passed through the hand from a plate on which the hand was resting. The conditioned stimulus was the ringing of a bell or the lighting of a colored lamp. Aged men, under these circumstances, took about twice as long to develop the conditioned hand retraction. It is also interesting to note that differentiation among unconditioned stimuli took longer in the older subjects; two very aged men failed to make the discrimination between a red and a yellow light.

Botwinick and Kornetsky (1960) studied conditioning and extinction of the galvanic skin response using electric shock as the unconditioned stimulus and a tone as the conditioned stimulus. The 39 older subjects extinguished their response to the tone without pairing with shock more readily than the nine young controls. Also, the elderly subjects conditioned less readily. The authors concluded that the older subjects were less reactive. The basis for a lowered reactivity on the part of older subjects is not established. The lowered reactivity may be an adaptive phenomenon with age or it may be a result of an endogenously reduced neural activity. Regardless of their ultimate basis, the findings have implications for conditions of human learning, particularly learning of speeded perceptual tasks. The conditions of stimulus presentation must be carefully controlled so the older subject is exposed to the stimulus with equal intensity. In a more general way the attention of older subjects may have to be "shaped up" more explicitly to equalize the task compared with young subjects, i.e., learning should be analyzed holding constant conditions of stimulus input for the age groups.

It should be pointed out that the studies of Botwinick and Kornetsky used subjects with a mean age over 70 years. In the case of Braun and Geiselhart's study, their subjects also had a mean age of 70 years. When Marinesco and Kreindler referred to the fact that they couldn't establish a certain type of trace conditioned reflexes in older subjects they were discussing eight subjects between the ages of 75 and 90 years. Certainly in this age range it is quite reasonable to be suspicious of the success in excluding deteriorative disease states as influencing the course of the conditioning, rather than an intrinsic change with age in the plasticity of the nervous system itself. It is of interest that the age range studied by the experimental psychologist and physiologist frequently lies considerably above the range ordinarily of interest to the adult educator. For this reason it is important to keep in mind what age group is being referred to in statements about older individuals.

These and other results of conditioning and learning studies may have some bearing upon the notions of set elaborated by Botwinick (1959). It is more difficult to arouse the same set or expectancy for a stimulus and to maintain this state of expectancy over long intervals in the older person.

Set or Expectancy

One of the relevant conditions in learning is the focus of the subject's attention or the intensity with which the individual expects a stimulus. Botwinick has shown that there is a difference with age in the expectancy for sound signals in simple reaction time experiments. Older persons perform at their fastest when the sound signal, to which a reaction is to be made by lifting a finger, occurs at a regular interval after a warning signal. Under the circumstances of a regular preparatory interval between a warning signal and a stimulus, older subjects are at their relative best in speed of response. This would suggest that the conditions of the stimulus may be designed to maximize expectancy and likely modify the intensity of the registered event in learning situations. The use of regular warning signals and preset intervals prior to associated stimuli can minimize tendencies to distraction or irrelevant associations occurring during the course of learning studies. In its broadest aspect, set or expectancy to learn may be a matter of long standing habit, that is, the better educated subject has learned how to learn and has a set or expectancy to approach novel stimulus situations with a strategy in mind. The older subject may not have a set to develop a strategy for seeking out the crucial elements in a learning task and for concentrating on these rather than on irrelevant features. It may well be that years since school does effect one's expectancy to learn and ability to seek out the crucial elements in a learning situation. Here again, however, one is giving emphasis to a para-learning variable, i.e., a variable not intrinsic to the process of acquisition *per se* but to a condition which governs the intensity of registration of important task elements.

One of the intriguing issues in relation to set or attitude, has been the possibility that older subjects are resistant to change, i.e., all things being equal, the older individual may be less willing to try new activities. Chown defined rigidity as, " . . . lack of change of behavior, where a change is necessary for success at the task, and where the subject knows that a change is likely to be demanded" (1961). She found individual differences in five distinct kinds of rigidity: spontaneous flexibility, disposition rigidity, personality rigidity, speed, and alphabet rigidity. Her results were based upon 16 tests of rigidity and 2 intelligence tests given to 200 men over the age range 20-80 years. In order of magnitude of variance, the effects of general intelligence were largest, then age, and then spontaneous flexibility. Age and general intelligence were closely associated, and between them accounted for 30 per cent of the total variance. The factors of rigidity, conceived of as independent of intelligence, seem discrete and of much smaller magnitude. Certainly there is no evidence here for invoking a concept of general behavioral rigidity in explaining test performance of older persons. Rather it is more reasonable to regard the constraints of behavior as primarily cognitive in nature and secondarily as due to rigidity of minor specialized sorts. It is noted that with age the effects of speed became more diffuse in Chown's data, again suggesting that the speed factor with advancing age tends towards a more pervasive factor rather than task specific in nature.

Brinley (1962) made a comprehensive study of the relation of age to performance of 21 speed tests (versions of word, number, and perceptual-spatial tests). Rigidity was operationally defined as the additional time required to do a mixed task (alternation task) compared with time to do a non-shift task. In each of the non-shift tasks the subject successively performed one type of operation; there were three different single operations in each of the categories. The shift task alternated all three operations. In the sense that older subjects (59-82 years) took more time than the young (18-36 years) on the shift tasks, the older subjects exhibited greater rigidity or inflexibility. However, both from results of a factor analysis and from an analysis of average trends, the performance of the older subjects on the alternation tasks was predictable from performance of non-shift tasks. Thus it was not necessary to invoke a new variable (rigidity) to explain slower performance under shift conditions. As in other studies (Birren, et al., 1962), a general speed factor, associated with accuracy, was found in the older group but not in the young. Speed was positively correlated with accuracy in the older group. The findings led Brinley to conclude that the speed of performance of older subjects is a measure of the extent to which the subject(s) maintains effective control over his cognitive sets. While older subjects would appear slower in task performance when different tasks are mixed, one apparently may not infer that the characteristic is other than cognitive, e.g., that it is attitudinal or affective in basis.

One should distinguish the willingness to be exposed to a new experience from the capacity to focus attention on that which is to be learned. This point may be examined by comparing incidental and intentional learning conditions as was done by Wimer (1960). The task was to associate six different words (middle, agile, gloomy, sturdy, cautious, and wicked) with the color in which they were printed (green, red, yellow, turquoise, orange, and violet). In one experimental condition subjects were told they were going to be asked later about the colors, in the other condition subjects were merely told that the procedure was a study of the effects of color upon reading speed. Under the latter condition, the subject is unfocused rather than set to learn. Wimer had 15 subjects over 65, and 17 subjects under 30 learn the word-color relationship. There was a significant age difference in learning under the intentional conditions but not under the incidental conditions. Why older subjects showed comparable incidental learning but not intentional learning is not readily explained. This study, while by no means conclusive, suggests that the role of set and attention, so well developed by Botwinick and Brinley in speed of performance of simple tasks, should be examined in relation to the learning context for older subjects.

Logical Problem Solving

Jerome (1960) reported a preliminary study of age differences in logical problem solving. While his rather automated experimental method showed age differences in problem solving activity, of perhaps greater interest was the attempt to localize within the activity the source of the differences. Jerome's subjects were rather well educated. There were 12 young women, mean age 23 years, most of whom were college students, and 11 retired government employees or their wives, mean age 66 years (range 60-85), most of whom were at least high school graduates. Among the latter were a chemist, three engineers, and a retired editor, representing higher maximum educational achievement than that found in the young group. The younger subjects produced more satisfactory results from fewer questions in the task. Older subjects asked four or five times as many redundant questions as the younger ones. There is the implication that the older subjects did not have explicit knowledge of the goal of a particular problem until late in the exploratory effort. Jerome concluded, "What the present study indicates, then, is that the patterns of heuristic behavior, so laboriously built up during youth through formal education and emulation of skilled acquaintances, decay with age. What seems to decay is a certain facility for recognizing occasions for the application of heuristically controlled behavior." The age difference in performance observed by Jerome may reflect a change in set or expectancy away from the employment of a rational strategy, in favor of a subjective or idiosyncratic associative approach to problems.

Interference Effects

One of the long standing issues in relation to age and learning is the possibility that with increasing age there is a greater likelihood of interference of past habits with present learning. It is perhaps not implausible that the acquisition of many years of experience and habits tends to intrude irrelevant content into new learning situations. With a greater amount of experience an increased probability of negative transfer is predicted in learning situations. Ruch (1934) carried out one of the earliest experiments designed to examine some of the effects of age on reorganization of long established behavior patterns. In one experiment he used a rotary pursuit task. One task condition used direct vision whereas another used mirror vision introducing a conflict and a considerable reorganization of visual motor habits. With the assumption of a greater consolidation of visual motor habits in older persons one is led to expect that this reversal situation should produce greater decrements in the performance of older persons. Under the conditions of the mirror reversal, older subjects showed a relatively poorer performance than they did in the direct-view situation. It should be noted that there were only trivial differences in the performance of subjects age 12-17 compared with ages 34-59. The older subjects in these studies were 60-82. Again, age in this sense is outside the range normally considered in adult education. In this instance of mirror reversal it need not be the long standing visual-motor habits which are interfering but rather if kinesthetic imagery is weaker in older persons, then their greater reliance upon vision necessarily leads to a disproportionate interference in the reversal situation. That is, it is not the undue proaction of habit patterns so much as it is a necessary dependence upon certain perceptual elements in the task or task context.

Ruch also studied interference effects using word associates and nonsense and false equations. An adaptation of this work by Korchin and Basowitz (1958) failed to duplicate the finding that interference materials are more difficult for older persons. It is quite possible that interference in learning in relation to age is quite dependent upon the relative extent of perceptual, motor, and symbolic conflict, perhaps being least in the latter category.

Gladis and Braun (1958) studied the effects of age on learning and recall of paired associates in a study that was designed to produce marked interference effects. In this study five lists of paired associates were given. After the initial learning, each subject learned two eight-term paired associate lists with successive words. These words had varying degrees of similarity in meaning to the original learning or paired associates. Each subject learned the original list of paired associates two minutes after he learned one of the interpolated lists of words of varying relationships; two minutes subsequent to this he began the relearning of the original materials. In all instances the lists were learned to the criterion of a perfect trial each. The data of this study are presented in Table 10. Jerome (1959) pointed out that the analysis of these

Table 10

Average Learning Rate and Recall Scores for Paired-Associates in Several Age Groups. (Gladis and Braun, 1958, adapted)

	Age Groups		
	20 to 29	40 to 49	60 to 72
Mean Raw Scores			
Original Learning	14.8	19.7	23.3
Interpolated Learning	10.9	15.2	17.7
Gains	3.9	4.5	5.6
Recall	4.3	4.0	3.3
Transformed Scores			
Original Learning	79.98	59.65	53.30
Interpolated Learning	116.88	80.88	72.30
Gains	36.90	21.23	19.00
Adjusted Scores			
Original Learning	85.78	59.18	48.10
Interpolated Learning	112.23	83.48	73.81
Gains	26.45	24.30	25.71
Recall	3.90	4.14	3.52

data indicated that there is a superiority in absolute amount of transfer for the older subjects when the raw scores are considered. This, however, became a reliable superiority in favor of youth when the scores were transformed to reciprocals and adjusted for vocabulary and rate of original learning. Botwinick has already pointed out some of the problems of interpretation of this data (1959). Since the vocabulary normally increases with age, the proper method of equating young and old subjects in verbal learning experiments is problematic. In terms of verbal comprehension, older people on the average should be expected to know more words than their counterpart as young adults. What appears from the study is that the transfer effect depends upon the kinds of controls one uses in the learning situation, i.e., rate of original learning and the matching of subjects. Such kinds of interference effects are obtained ideally under laboratory conditions and may not correspond to what people have in mind, however, when they speak of interference effects of life-long habits.

Speed and Learning

Equally difficult as the tearing apart of motivation and learning is the task of separating the influence of speed of performance on learning (Birren, et al., 1962). With their greater speed, younger subjects can attempt more trials per unit time and it may be expected as a result that they will also show greater learning per unit time. This suggests that the relation of learning and practice ought to be closely examined for the amount of practice per unit time. Speed of performance may also affect the amount of learning per attempt in older subjects by separating the rewards or knowledge of results from attempts giving a lessened reinforcement effect. It should not be concluded from these remarks about the necessity to separate performance speed from learning that these two processes could not be intrinsically related, that is, the ability of the organism to perform quickly under certain conditions may be associated with the plasticity of behavior independent of the increased exposure of the organism to learning per unit time. One must be cautious, however, in view of the void of information on the optimum conditions for the distribution of practice in different age groups, the timing of reinforcements or, in complex tasks, the provision for knowledge of results all of which may differentially affect the learning of adults of different ages.

Animal Studies

Animal learning studies in relation to age should be less quoted for their direct relevance to phenomena of human learning than as models of experimental analysis. The studies of Verzar-McDougall (1957) indicate that the age deficit in learning in rats may not be uniformly distributed in the population. She had rats of different ages learn a multiple T-maze to obtain a food reward. Her learning criterion was not more than three total errors in three consecutive runs. As a group, the older animals showed inferior learning in a maze. However, she did point out that half of the rats in the age range 12-27 months learned the maze equally well as the young adult rats of 8-9 months, implying, as did the earlier cited human studies, that the deficit condition affecting rat learning is not continuously distributed in the population. A follow-up study of this learning experiment indicated that those rats which showed inferior retention had a greater probability of greater cell loss in the frontal lobes of the brain.

Earlier studies by Stone (1929) using a multiple discrimination box did not show age differences in learning by rats over the age range 31-770 days. At each point of five choices in the discrimination box, the rat has to choose an exit through one of two windows. The correct window was that which was illuminated on a given trial.

A study of learning in the rat using a swimming tank and a two-choice maze was carried out by Birren (1962). Little evidence was obtained in this study of a deficit in the older rat to learn the two-choice maze. The study added the further point that when animals were matched for initial ability to learn, reversal of the two-choice situation did not produce any greater interference for the older animal (Figure 4). One aspect of this study which did show a deficit in learning of the older rat, involved the greater tendency of older rats to swim back and forth along the side wall of the tank thus avoiding a choice situation. This was interpreted as indicating a long-standing habit on the part of the older rat to cling to a wall as a type of tropism. This is perhaps another example of a secondary interference with the learning process. By analogy to the adult human one must also be cautious about a greater dependence upon one sensory system because of a diminished acuity in another. What appears to be a deficit in learning may merely be a necessity to depend to an excessive extent upon information via one modality. Whereas the rat with advancing age may come to depend more and more upon tactile and kinesthetic orientation, the adult human appears to be increasingly dependent upon vision (Welford, 1958).

The studies by Kay and Sime (1961) also lend themselves to the interpretation that while learning performance of rats may differ with age

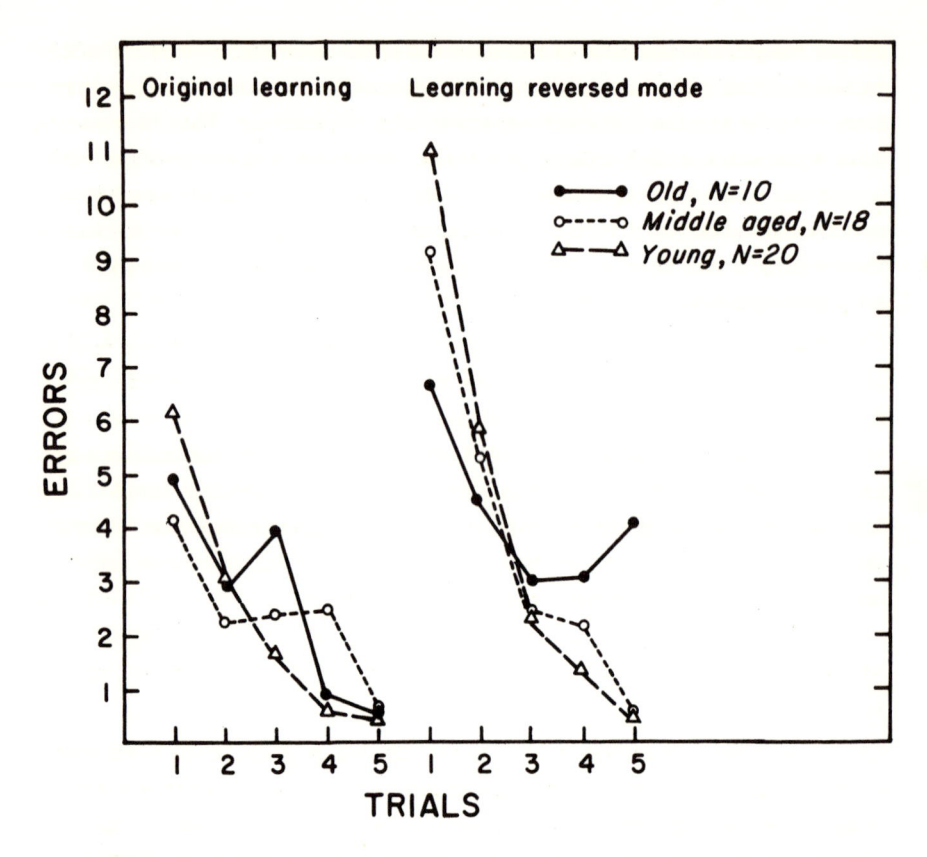

Figure 4. Mean errors per trial by rats in three age groups (young 2-3 months; middle-aged 12 months; old 24-26 months) for original learning and reversal learning. Age groups were equated for original learning (Birren, 1962).

under some conditions, the difference may be attributed to perceptual rather than to intrinsic learning change. Certainly one must at least conclude from the studies of aging and learning in rats that there is no learning deficit regularly seen. When deficits of learning performance occur, they are more likely due to a change in some para-learning variable, such as perception, motivation, or senile debilitation not typical of all animals.

Summary

Less is known about the characteristics of adult learners and the optimum conditions for learning than about children and young adults. One major reason for the lack of information about learning by mature adults is the fact that they are less frequently bound in situations where objective records are kept of their progress of performance. This is changing somewhat since a high rate of industrial innovations are occurring with a reduced emphasis on psychomotor skills, and with greater emphasis on academic subject matter. Learning and retraining of adults throughout the employed life span will very likely be a characteristic feature of future employment.

Pilot studies of adult learning in automated industry indicate that for many if not most tasks, years of education is a more relevant variable than chronological age. There has been a marked tendency in research in recent years (since the work of Thorndike in 1928) to advance the age at which subjects are regarded as old in studies of learning. Old for most laboratory studies means a group with a mean age over seventy years. One factor in the advance in the age at which adult learners are regarded as old is the rise in average educational attainment of the population over successive decades. Most persons in the upper age range of employment are able to participate in learning in industry because of adequate educational background.

The evidence which has been accumulating on both animal and human learning suggests that age changes in primary ability to learn are small under most circumstances. When significant age differences in learning appear, they seem more readily attributed to processes of perception, set, attention, motivation, and the physiological state of the organism, including that of disease. Possible exceptions to this generalization appear to be classical conditioning and psychomotor skills, although even in these exceptions which show age differences in learning the crucial variable may be attention or set. Further studies are clearly needed on the way to "shape up" attention and set in the older learner, and encourage the development of learning strategies which may fall into disuse as a consequence of years since leaving school. Since attention and set are implicated, it would seem that programed learning using mechanical and optical devices is worthy of study in relation to age. Older adults may gain relatively more than the young from a programed learning context which closely controls attention and reduces irrelevant stimuli as well providing immediate knowledge of results.

Limitations of mental test performance and learning can arise from changes in health associated with the development of disease, e.g., cerebrovascular or cardiovascular disease. Individual differences in health appear to be a significant contributor to individual differences in mental abilities of older adults. Data even suggest that length of life is to some extent related to mental test performance.

Given good education and good health there is little reason to expect an involution of the capacity to learn over the conventional period of employment. The use of this capacity implies adequate motivation and personal adjustment, which is not always the case in older as in young adults (see discussion by Kuhlen, 1959). The use of the capacity to learn also implies available opportunity for continuing learning under the guidance of adult educators who are able to provide the optimum conditions in which to learn.

References

Bayley, Nancy, and Oden, Melita H. The maintenance of intellectual ability in gifted adults. J. Geront., 1955, 10, 91-107.

Bilash, I., and Zubek, J. P. The effects of age on factorially "pure" mental abilities. J. Geront., 1960, 15, 175-82.

Birren, J. E., Botwinick, J., Weiss, A. D., and Morrison, D. F. An analysis of mental and perceptual tests given to healthy elderly men. In, A Study of Human Aging: Biological and Psychological Aspects. (In press, 1962).

Birren, J. E. Age differences in learning a two-choice water maze by rats. J. Geront., 1962, 17, 207-13.

Birren, J. E., and Morrison, D. F. Analysis of the WAIS subtests in relation to age and education. J. Geront., 1961, 16, 363-69.

Birren, J. E., Riegel, K. F., and Morrison, D. F. Age differences in response speed as a function of controlled variations of stimulus conditions: evidence of a general speed factor. Gerontologia, 1962, 6, 1-18.

Botwinick, J. Drives, expectancies, and emotions. In, Handbook of Aging and the Individual, J. E. Birren, ed., Chicago: University of Chicago Press, 1959, Chapter 21, pp. 739-68.

Botwinick, J., and Kornetsky, C. Age differences in the acquisition and extinction of the GSR. J. Geront., 1960, 15, 83-84.

Botwinick, J., Brinley, J. F., and Robbin, J. S. Learning a position discrimination and position reversals by Sprague-Dawley rats of different ages. J. Geront., 1960, 15, 315-19.

Botwinick, J., and Brinley, J. F. Aspects of RT set during brief intervals in relation to age and sex. J. Geront., 1960, 15, 295-301.

Braun, H. W., and Geiselhart, R. Age differences in the acquisition and extinction of the conditioned eyelid response. J. exper. Psychol., 1959, 57, 386-88.

Brinley, J. F. Rigidity and the control of cognitive sets in relation to age differences in speed and accuracy of performance. Doctoral Dissertation, Department of Psychology, Catholic University, Washington, D.C.

Chown, Sheila M. Age and the rigidities. J. Geront., 1961, 16, 353-62.

Clark, J. W. The aging dimension: a factorial analysis of individual differences with age on psychological and physiological measurements. J. Geront., 1960, 15, 183-87.

Falek, A., Kallmann, F. J., Lorge, I., and Jarvik, Lissy F. Longevity and intellectual variation in a senescent twin population. J. Geront., 1960, 15, 305-9.

Gladis, M., and Braun, H. W. Age differences in transfer and retroaction as a function of intertask response similarity. J. exper. Psychol., 1958, 55, 25-30.

Jarvik, Lissy F., Kallmann, F. J., and Falek, A. Intellectual changes in aged twins. J. Geront., 1960, 15, 289-94.

Jerome, E. A. Age and learning-experimental studies. In, Handbook of Aging and the Individual, J. E. Birren, ed., Chicago: University of Chicago Press, 1959, Chapter 19, pp. 655-99.

Jerome, E. A. Decay of heuristic processes in the aged. (In press, 1962.)

Jones, H. E. Intelligence and problem-solving. In, Handbook of Aging and the Individual, J. E. Birren, ed., Chicago: University of Chicago Press, 1959, Chapter 20, pp. 700-38.

Kay, H. Theories and learning and aging. In, Handbook of Aging and the Individual, J. E. Birren, ed., Chicago: University of Chicago Press, 1959, Chapter 18, pp. 614-54.

Kay, H., and Sime, M. Discrimination learning with old and young rats. J. Geront., 1962, 17, 75-80.

Kleemeier, R. W. Age changes in mental abilities in the senium. July, 1961. Unpublished address at the American Psychological Association meeting.

Korchin, S., and Basowitz, H. Age differences in verbal learning. J. abnorm. soc. Psychol., 1957, 54, 64-69.

Kuhlen, R. G. Aging and life-adjustment. In, Handbook of Aging and the Individual, J. E. Birren, ed., Chicago: University of Chicago Press, 1959, Chapter 24, pp. 852-97.

Marinesco, G., and Kreindler, A. Des réflexes conditionnels, troisième parties: application des réflexes conditionnels à certains problèmes cliniques. J. Psychol., 1934, 31, 722-91.

Obrist, W. D., Busse, E. W., Eisdorfer, C., and Kleemeier, R. W. Relation of the electroencephalogram to intellectual function in senescence. J. Geront., 1962, 17, 197-206.

Owens, W. A. Age and mental abilities. Genet. Psychol. Monogr., 1953, 48, 3-54.

Reed, H. B. C., Jr., and Reitan, R. M. The significance of age in the performance of a complex psychomotor task by brain-damaged and non-brain-damaged subjects. J. Geront., 1962, 17, 193-96.

Riegel, K. F. A study of verbal achievements of older persons. J. Geront., 1959, 14, 453-56.

Ruch, F. L. The differentiative effect of age upon learning. J. gen. Psychol., 1934, 11, 261-86.

Sanderson, R. E., and Inglis, J. Learning and mortality in elderly psychiatric patients. J. Geront., 1961, 16, 375-76.

Sime, M., and Kay, H. Inter-problem interference and age. J. Geront., 1962, 17, 81-87.

Stone, C. P. The age factor in animal learning. Genet. Psychol. Monogr., 1929, 5, & 6.

Thorndike, E. L., Bregman, E. O., Tilton, J. W., and Windward, E. Adult Learning. New York: Macmillan Co., 1928.

Verzar-McDougall, E. J. Studies in learning and memory in aging rats. Gerontologia, 1957, 1, 65-85.

U.S. Department of Labor. Industrial retraining programs for technological change, a study of the performance of older workers. Washington, D.C.: Government Printing Office. (In press.)

U.S. Department of Labor. Adjustments to the introduction of office automation. Washington, D.C.: Government Printing Office, Bulletin 1276, May, 1960.

Welford, A. T. Aging and Human Skill. London: Oxford University Press, 1958.

Wimer, R. E. Age differences in incidental and intentional learning. J. Geront., 1960, 15, 79-82.

III

PERSONALITY CHANGES DURING THE ADULT YEARS[1]

Bernice L. Neugarten
Committee on Human Development
University of Chicago

The focus of this paper is upon adult personality as it is seen from the perspective of the student of human development. Human development is becoming increasingly well-delineated within the behavioral sciences as a line of inquiry that is not identical with that of psychology, not even with that of developmental psychology. The student of human development is interested primarily in the behavior of normal persons and representative samples of persons, rather than in clinical cases or in deviant groups; in behavior as it occurs within the real-life situation, rather than in the experimental situation; with the relationships between complex sets of variables, social and biological, as well as psychological; and, above all, with the ways in which these relationships vary with time throughout the life span.

Personality is viewed in dynamic terms, as a set of processes that have a course of growth and change from earliest childhood through old age. The adult personality is seen as continuous but not identical with the personality of the child and the adolescent. In seeking ways to describe how the adult differs from the child, the investigator is well-advised to focus his attention upon the importance of the "self," and upon those elements in the personality that involve choice, self-direction, and the manipulation of outcomes. Personality is to be studied, then, as a set of independent variables in accounting for human behavior. From this perspective, very little is known about adult personality. There are few theories to guide those of us who are investigators; despite the hundreds of studies that are concerned with one or another aspect of personality, there are few empirical studies that can be used to guide those of us who

---

1. Prepared with the assistance of Mr. Mark Skinner.

are adult educators. Our knowledge of the personality changes that occur in adulthood is scanty for various reasons.

Problems of Method

First there are problems related to method. The problems of sampling alone become increasingly acute as we move through the age-range. We lose the captive research groups available in nurseries, schools, and colleges; adults have different, often decreasing, motivation for participating in research projects; and as investigators we are aware that, as the age of our subjects increases, we must be increasingly wary about generalizing from what may be deviant to normal groups (such as generalizing from volunteers to non-volunteers, or from the institutionalized to the non-institutionalized aged).

There is the difficulty also that the rhythm of change is different in adulthood from that in childhood. A year, which is so long an interval in the early stages of life, is so short an interval in later life that we must use long time intervals as our units. Yet there is the difficulty that the longer our time intervals, or the more we separate our samples by chronological age in the attempt to highlight age differences, the more other characteristics will operate to confound the age variable itself. For instance, if we attempt to equate a group of 20-year-olds with a group of 40-year-olds with regard to educational level, we are likely to introduce systematic bias with regard to socioeconomic level. This bias grows in geometric proportion as we attempt to enlarge the age interval between groups.

To make matters worse, we cannot estimate the effects of survival bias, that is, what types of individuals have died, and what types, survived. Yet we know the effects of this bias become greater and greater at advanced ages, so that the problem of equating samples of young and old persons on grounds that they will be equally representative becomes, in most studies, nearly impossible.

If, furthermore, we are cautious about drawing inferences with regard to developmental changes from studies based on cross-sectional data, then we face the tremendous difficulties inherent in carrying out longitudinal research over the long time-intervals required to produce meaningful findings.

This is to say nothing of the difficulty involved in disentangling the effects of historical and secular changes in the society from the effects of increasing age: as, for example, when studies report an increase in conservative attitudes in successive age groups. Do persons become more conservative with age? Or is it that older persons formed many of their social attitudes at a different time in history? (It might be pointed out that there seem to be a growing number of middle-aged parents, who, having gone through their own formative period in the days of the New Deal, are appalled at the political conservatism in their young adult children.)

It is a rare instance in which a study can be designed to control for this factor—a study in which we make observations, say, on a group of persons when they are 20, and again when they are 40; in which we observe a second group who are 20 at the same time that the first group reaches 40; and in which we can then compare the Time 1-Time 2 difference with the Group 1-Group 2 difference.

Such problems of method, while they do not distinguish research in personality from research in many other areas, may nevertheless provide special hurdles to the student of personality processes. One problem does arise more often perhaps than in other areas: that is the problem of generalizing from behavior in the experimentally-controlled situation to behavior in the real-life situation. Without going into this issue at greater length, it can perhaps be argued that the problem becomes more acute with regard to adult behavior than with child behavior, for it is confounded by questions regarding suitable predictors in the lives of adults. What shall be the criteria in adulthood to which experimental findings be compared?

Problems of Theory

Over and above problems of method, however, the student of adult personality suffers from the lack of theory. Any investigator needs theory to guide him in making observations. Indeed, the very manner in which we conceptualize personality determines which phenomena we choose to consider, and the kinds of measures we attempt to devise.

Yet we are faced with a strange anomaly. Psychologists are becoming increasingly impressed with developmental issues, as witnessed in the growing rapprochement going on, for instance, between learning theory and psychoanalytic theory; and in another instance, between developmental theory and research in cognitive processes. Furthermore, most psychologists, and certainly most educators, are committed to the concepts of developmental change in children and in adolescents. By developmental is meant the view that although behavior is always molded by social transactions, growth and change are also inherent in the organism; and the view that the changes observable through time are dictated by a variety of factors, not all of them external.

This point of view, although it has been more elegantly stated by others, needs no elaboration when it refers to childhood and adolescence. We are accustomed to the thought that the child is not a tabula rasa; that there are inner processes and needs which change with time; and that the personality of the child cannot be accounted for solely on the basis of his social experiences.

For the most part, however, personality theorists have not carried the same view forward into adulthood. This is an over-simplification, of course, but by and large we have almost nothing that could be called a developmental theory of adulthood. Psychoanalytic theory, tremendous as its influence has been, has given little attention to personality change after the crises of adolescence have been mastered. The personality is generally regarded as stabilized (if not fixed) by the time early adulthood is reached; and there are few developmental psychologists who have extended their theories upward in the attempt to account for the perceivable changes in adult behavior.

These introductory remarks may explain in some degree why it is we should proceed cautiously in considering those aspects of the topic that follow here. I have chosen to discuss, first, the issue of stability or continuity of personality, for I assume it is a major issue to adult educators who are concerned with the effects of the educative experience over long time spans. In that connection, I shall comment briefly upon individual differences, an issue already very familiar to educators.

In the last part of this paper, I shall change focus and move away from issues per se to a tentative formulation of the nature of personality change in adulthood. The focus will be narrowed at that point to deal with change in certain intrapsychic processes, change which hopefully will be seen as relevant to questions of content in adult education.[2]

---

2. To minimize overlap between the present paper and others to be

Continuity of Personality Through Time

Stability of personality is a major issue to students of human development. Most of the empirical evidence with regard to stability has come thus far from studies of children and adolescents, and to that extent, it is only partially useful with regard to adulthood. It happens, however, that there are now appearing a number of reports of longitudinal data in which $\underline{S}$s have now reached their 30's, and in a few instances, their 40's.

Youth to Young Adulthood

I shall draw here from only the most recently reported studies of this type, some of which have not yet seen publication.

At the Institute of Human Development, University of California, longitudinal studies have been in process for more than 25 years, and data are available concerning some 300 persons who are now in their 30's and 40's. There are presently emerging from that body of data a number of empirical findings with regard to continuity of personality through the period of young adulthood.

In a study by Mussen (1961), for example, boys who were rated as more and less masculine were restudied when they were in their 30's. Those who had been low in masculinity in adolescence were found still to be low with regard to masculine interests and attitudes. The more masculine boys became the more masculine adults.

Tuddenham (1959), to take another example, interviewed 72 men and women in their early 30's who had been studied at length some 19 years earlier. He rated these young adults on 53 personality variables, some of them variables of observed behavior, others, of inferred drives. Correlations between Time 1 and Time 2 were positive, but very low (average $\underline{r}$ was .27 for men, and .24 for women). Although Tuddenham concluded that "there is clearly a significant measure of temporal stability in personality across the developmental span from early adolescence to mature adulthood," he concluded also that the correlations were much too low to permit individual prediction.

To take another example from the California studies: of 139 subjects

---

presented at this conference, I have omitted from this discussion studies of intelligence, of motor skills, of interest patterns, of motivation—all of them important aspects of personality.

who had been followed from birth through age 18 by Macfarlane, and who were then seen again 12 years later as 30-year-olds, early predictions appeared to be confirmed for certain personality make-ups, not for others. Although these particular data have not yet been processed quantitatively, it seems clear that the over-controlled, well-ordered, compulsive individuals tend to continue in that pattern, but a number who were hostile and dependent in childhood had grown up to be friendly and nurturant adults (Jones, 1960).

Jones (1958), in a report of the work of the Institute, generalized from various studies of physical, physiological, intellectual, and personality development. Consonant with the findings emerging from other research centers, his conclusions were that the problem of age trend consistency was a more difficult one in the area of personality than in the other areas, among other reasons because the same research approaches cannot be used with adults as with children and adolescents. In spite of numerous instances of consistency between adolescent and adult measures, overall measures of adult adjustment showed little relation to strength of adolescent drives.

Jones concluded: "The problem here may lie partly in the fact that over a long period behavioral consistency, when it occurs, may be countered by changes in the environment. The adaptive significance of a given behavior pattern can thus be interpreted only with reference to changing demands in the life situation" (1960).

In line with the interpretation that there is relatively little continuity of personality observable from adolescence to adulthood is the study made by Rohrer and his associates (Rohrer and Edmonson, 1960). They traced a large majority of the Negro adolescents who had been described by Davis and Dollard in the book Children of Bondage (1940); they reported in considerable detail on 20 of those cases who were seen again after an interval of 20 years. Although the findings were not treated quantitatively, the net effect of these case materials was to highlight the great diversity of adult life patterns, only partly predictable from observations made during adolescence.

Different investigators, however, have differing interpretations with regard to continuity of personality. Symonds (1961), for instance, studied 28 subjects who were 12-18 at Time 1; and who were retested after an interval of 13 years. He found what he regarded as high consistency in overt personality—such characteristics as aggressiveness in response to interviews and tests; a correlation of .54 between rankings at Time 1 and Time 2 for general adjustment; and even such marked persistence of phantasy themes as to enable the investigators to identify the narrator and to match stories told 13 years apart. Symonds felt he had demonstrated "the remarkable persistence of personality over a 13-year interval, and in particular, the fact that it is possible to estimate personality adjustment in later years from facts gathered about a person when he is adolescent."

Given such inconsistent points of view, it is perhaps pertinent to complicate the issue even further, and to point out that the question of continuity has often been over-simplified by being stated only in terms of test-retest agreement on the same measures. The question is usually phrased: is a specific response at Time 1 exhibited again at Time 2?

It is perhaps more meaningful to the student of human behavior to study antecedent-consequent relationships by asking the more complex questions concerning, not repetition, but derivation: <u>what</u> behaviors or what characteristics at Time 1 are predictive of <u>what</u> behaviors or what characteristics at Time 2?

Yet if we turn to studies of the latter type, the empirical findings are not necessarily more congruent. In one such study, for instance, in which adjustment was being predicted, Anderson (1960) gathered data on all the children within a Minnesota county who were enrolled in school from grade 4 to grade 12; then followed them up 5 to 7 years later, by which time some were in their 20's. He reports that, as is true in other longitudinal studies of youngsters, cognitive abilities (intelligence, skill, knowledge) weighed more heavily than measures of personality in predicting adjustment at Time 2. (Independent of the problems of continuity and prediction, but also important to the present discussion, is Anderson's statement that cognitive measures were what he calls "age-bound"—that is, scores increase as age increases; whereas personality measures were relatively "age-free.")

Kagan and Moss (1962) have just reported a major study based upon longitudinal data gathered at Fels Research Institute on a group of 71 men and women now in their 20's. Using interviews with parents, narrative reports, and behavior observations collected over the years, <u>S</u>s were rated on a set of personality variables with regard to characteristic behavior at four periods in their childhood: infancy to age 3, 3-6, 6-10, and 10-14.

A second investigator, with no knowledge of the earlier data, interviewed each young adult at length and made assessments of present personality. Taking the antecedent-consequent rather than the test-retest approach, and basing their interpretations upon correlations of the magnitude of .5 to .6, these investigators concluded: " . . . Many of the behaviors exhibited by the child aged 6-10, and a few during the age period, 3-6, were moderately good predictors of theoretically related behaviors during early adulthood. Passive withdrawal from stressful situations, dependency on family, ease-of-anger arousal, involvement in intellectual mastery, social interaction anxiety, sex-role identification, and pattern of sexual behavior in adulthood were each related to reasonably analogous behavioral dispositions during the early school years. . . . These results offer strong support for the generalization that aspects of adult personality begin to take form during early childhood."

Yet in another broadly-designed study concerned with the prediction of performance in young adulthood, the conclusions were different. Hess and Davis (Hess, 1961) have followed up 350 young men and women whom they had studied eight years earlier when these $\underline{S}$s were seniors in high school. Assessments of these young adults have been made with regard to work-related achievement, social integration into the adult society, and psycho-social identity.

In general these investigators were impressed with the difficulties in predicting performance in young adulthood from measures taken in adolescence. Although academic achievement in high school (school grades, but not IQ) was associated significantly with work-related achievement in young men, social experience and social skills in adolescence showed only low correlations with subsequent behavior in social, in work, or in identity areas. Looking backward in time, furthermore, the measures of ego-identity established for these young adults were not consistently related to high school experience. In particular, measures of ego functions taken from projective tests of personality showed no significant correlations from Time 1 to Time 2.

These findings were true for the group as a whole, although more positive and consistent relationships between personality and achievement measures were found for the one-third of the group who fell at the extremes (those who were high achievers or low achievers at both Time 1 and Time 2).

Hess and Davis concluded not only that adult performance is apparently more closely related to events and experiences that occur after high school than to high school behavior (college attendance was the most significant factor); but that the high school years may constitute a kind of moratorium, and that it may be the transition from late adolescence into the 20's that is a more critical period of development than is adolescence.

It may be relevant at this point to comment upon the problems that arise in generalizing from samples which differ in heterogeneity. The Hess-Davis study of young adults was based on a group of 350, all of whom graduated from high school—a relatively homogeneous group. Havighurst and his associates (1962), on the other hand, in still another recently reported study, tested all children in the 6th grade in a midwestern town (including children in public and parochial schools, the mentally retarded as well as the normal) and then examined them again nine years later, when they were 20. Substantial correlations with adjustment at 20 were obtained for Time 1 measures of socioeconomic status, IQ, social leadership, and social adjustment as measured by the California Psychological Inventory (rs were .48 to .58). Adjustment at 20 was based upon ratings of educational progress, job success, marital success, and personal competence. These investigators conclude, somewhat contrary to Hess and Davis, that, given many exceptions, there is measurable continuity of personality. Children who are endowed with advantages make the most of these advantages during adolescence and become the most competent young adults.

These discrepant conclusions illustrate the difficulties involved in generalizing about continuity of personality. There is variation from study to study, not only with regard to size and heterogeneity of sample, but also with regard to the interval between Time 1 and Time 2. Perhaps predictions can be made more accurately from late childhood to young adulthood than from adolescence to young adulthood. Perhaps adolescence is itself too unstable a period in development to provide a good base line. If so, this might account for at least some of the discrepancies cited.

Another reason for the difficulties in evaluating the extent of consistency in personality through time is the fact that sometimes the focus has been upon the relatively overt, observable levels of behavior; at other times, upon the relatively covert, intrapsychic levels. To borrow terms from the biologist, the focus is at times upon phenotypic aspects of personality; at other times, upon genotypic. The same underlying trait can take a variety of overt forms; sometimes it is this fact that plays havoc with the best-designed study. It is not always easy to move from phenotypic behavior at Time 1 to an accurate conceptualization of the genotypic trait that underlies it; and from that conceptualization to a different measure of phenotypic behavior appropriate to Time 2. It is this difficulty that may also account for some of the discrepancies.

I have chosen to illustrate at some length from these studies of young adulthood. Given the difficulties in generalizing from longitudinal studies alone to even one age period, it is apparent how much greater the difficulties will be as the time perspective is lengthened in subsequent sections of this paper. Our knowledge of human development is as yet marked more by the absence than by the presence of clear and consistent findings. This is particularly the case with regard to personality; it is even more the case with regard to the adult personality.

Young to Middle Adulthood

The fact has been mentioned that in most centers for research in human development where longitudinal studies are in progress, subjects have not yet reached the middle years. As a consequence, there are very few sets of findings available with regard to continuity of personality from young- to middle-adulthood—or, for that matter, from any preceding period of time to the period of middle age.

There is the notable exception of the Terman and Oden study (1959) in which Terman's group of gifted children have been followed into their late 40's. These were some 1,500 children who, in 1921, were in the top one per cent of the population in IQ. The data on personality have not been systematically treated with regard to continuity, nor have they been reported in terms of successive time intervals. However, the latest follow-up, after three and a half decades, has shown that, with few exceptions, the superior child has become the able adult, superior in nearly every aspect to the average person. From this point of view, and in these very gross terms, the findings support the generalization of continuity through time.

An interesting point, although not directly related to the issue of continuity, is the investigators' conclusion that relates to the importance of personality factors in adult achievement. On the criteria of eminence, professional status, and recognized position in the community, the 150 most successful and the 150 least successful men were isolated from among this group of gifted subjects. The two subgroups differed most widely on four personality traits: persistence in the accomplishment of ends, integration toward goals, self-confidence, and freedom from inferiority feelings. In general, the investigators conclude, the greatest contrast between the two groups was in all-around emotional and social adjustment and in the drive to achieve. These findings suggest again the central importance, and perhaps the relative independence of personality factors as research variables in human behavior.

The second notable exception is the Kelly study (1955), in which 300 engaged couples were first studied in the 1930's and then re-tested in 1955 when they were in their 40's. After correcting the correlations for attenuation, Kelly found that individual consistency was highest in the areas of values and vocational interests ($\underline{r}$s were approximately .50); and was low but statistically significant with regard to self-ratings and other personality variables based upon responses to paper-and-pencil tests. (These latter coefficients were of the order of .30.) Kelly leaves open the question of whether or not these findings should be interpreted as signifying high or low consistency. However, he does point out that there is obviously a great amount of individual variation, and he concludes: "Our findings indicate that significant changes in the human personality may continue to occur during the years of adulthood."

Middle to Old Age

The degree to which we can speak of continuity when one moves from middle to old age is even more open to question. There are, so far as I know, no longitudinal studies on personality for individuals who have been studied in young adulthood, or in middle adulthood, and then again in old age.

It has often been commented on by clinicians that the personality structure becomes more clearly revealed as individuals grow old; that the person seems to grow "more like himself." Dr. Martin Gumpert, a well-known geriatrician, said: "With age, the outline of a psyche becomes more apparent." Yet there is little in the way of controlled investigation to demonstrate whether or not this observation is true.

Our findings about personality change in old age are drawn from cross-sectional data; and strictly speaking, we have no systematic evidence regarding individual consistency over long periods of time when time relates to the latter half of the life span.

We shall move in a moment to findings from cross-sectional data; but meanwhile, what should we conclude with regard to continuity of personality in the adult years? Granted that most of the empirical findings refer to the first part of adulthood, there are nevertheless certain points that bear restatement:

1. Test-retest on single variables or on sets of variables may not, indeed, provide the most meaningful approach to the problem of continuity. Any given trait, such as aggressiveness in males or expressivity in females, however the trait may be measured, may have quite different significance at Time 1 and Time 2 when seen within a wider pattern of variables. The individual may maintain his relative position on a given characteristic. This fact may be less important than the way in which that characteristic is related to other characteristics at the two points in time. In this connection, for example, clinical observations have been frequently made that aggressivity may be adaptive in youth, but maladaptive in middle age; just as rigidity may be maladaptive in young adulthood, but adaptive in old age.

The more worthwhile question might be one to which certain of the longitudinal studies cited here have already been addressed: namely, what are the predictors at Time 1 for a particular trait or constellation of traits at Time 2? If, for instance, we wish to understand the antecedents of personal adjustment in middle age, to what variables should we attend when individuals are young adults? To carry this example further, there are a number of studies which indicate that intelligence or cognitive ability is perhaps the most powerful predictor of personal adjustment when Time 1 and Time 2 refer to childhood and adolescence, or to adolescence and young adulthood. The picture is not so clear, however, when we move beyond young adulthood. That is, it is not clear whether or not intelligence is a powerful predictor of personal adjustment at later ages.[3]

---
3. A study in this connection is one by Mulvey (1961), who studied the career patterns of several hundred middle-aged women, all of whom had graduated from high school, and who concluded that, of a variety of

2. Whether the studies are test-retest or predictive in design (in the sense described earlier), the general picture with regard to consistency of adult personality can be summarized by saying that measures taken at long time intervals tend to produce statistically reliable, but relatively low, correlations. (Coefficients are usually of the order of .30 to .40, only occasionally are they as high as .50.) The indication is that while there is indeed continuity of personality that is measurable by our present techniques, the larger proportion of the variance in our measures at Time 2 remains unaccounted for. Put in less technical terms (and making allowance for fallibility), the implication is that there is at least as much change as there is stability. From this perspective alone, if from no other, we are justified in proceeding with the topic before us. The <u>nature</u> of personality changes in adulthood may be relatively obscure; but the conviction is a reasonable one that changes do indeed occur.

Empirical studies such as those cited here capture only part of the complexity of human behavior. From one point of view, this is so obvious a point that I apologize for stating it. Yet investigators sometimes overlook the obvious in pinning their sights upon the empirical, the controlled, and the experimental methods of observation. We all know that people change in personality as they grow older.

Every individual, as he moves through the adult years, becomes transformed in his appearance, in his social life patterns, his interests, his personal and social relationships—in what might be called outward or observable characteristics. It is also highly probable that individuals change through the years of adulthood with regard to inner qualities of personality—for example, in ways of experiencing and expressing emotions, in motivations, in preoccupations—in the whole array of cognitive and affective processes that are involved in the day's traffic with the environment. One has only to think of the waking, as well as the dreaming, thoughts that preoccupied him ten years ago, and the thoughts that preoccupy him now, to see that this is so.

Individual Differences

Intimately related to the question of continuity is the question of the extent to which individuals may be expected to vary, one from another,

---

factors measured in youth, intelligence was the least important in influencing the kinds of career lines that ensued.

with increasing age. In some ways a developmental point of view leads us to search for patterns that are common to all members of a group, or for what we euphemistically refer to as "laws" of growth and change. Studies of childhood and adolescence have focused on this problem. On the other hand, longitudinal studies have also highlighted individual variation in growth patterns.

It is not clear to what extent the periods of adulthood and old age show the same general relationships between common patterns and idiosyncratic patterns as are shown in childhood—in other words, to what extent all people are alike and to what extent they are all different, once the period of growth is over.

From the biologist's point of view, the forces of natural selection—if they may still be said to apply, in our man-made environment—are no longer operative once the reproductive period of life is over. If a trait is neither biologically adaptive nor non-adaptive for the species, in the sense that it does not affect the rate of reproduction (a trait related to senescence, as compared with a trait related to growth), then it does not become eliminated from the population. It may be, therefore, that a greater variety of patterns develop in the last half of life than in the first half; and the more that man controls the effects of natural selection by creating a protective environment for less hardy biological specimens, the more variation we can expect in older organisms.

Within the social and cultural realms, we can expect differences between individuals to be accentuated with time, as educational, vocational and social events accumulate one after another to create more and more differentiated sets of experiences from one person to the next.

Whatever the net effects of these factors might be; and making allowance for the extent to which common social roles lead to increased similarities and therefore to greater homogeneity, it is not unreasonable to expect that variation will increase as a group of persons moves from youth through adulthood. There is the factor of personal choice; and the factor of ever-increasing differentiation, once initial choices are made in one or another direction. There are also the ever-increasing effects of personal commitments and institutional structures that tend to produce increased individual differences between persons. Any high-school class may be said to be more alike at the time of graduation than at age 25, 40, or 60 in life patterns, interests, and abilities; so also is it likely, if appropriate measurements are obtainable, that the members would prove to be more similar in personality at the time of graduation.

It is a fact, on the other hand, that if one looks at empirical studies that are presently available, the picture with regard to increased differentiation with age is not so clear. Some studies indicate greater individual differences with increasing age; some do not.

There are major problems in interpreting these empirical findings, for the actual age groups being compared differ from study to study. In one case 20-year-olds are being compared with 40-year-olds; in another, with 60-year-olds. Above all, samples tend to be poorly controlled.

For the educator, it may be the best policy to proceed on the assumption that adults can be expected to vary more greatly than children in personality, just as in other areas; and that these differences are likely to be greater, the older the clients he attempts to serve. This is likely to be true, at least, until the very oldest age group, when biological decrements may operate to narrow the range of behavior.

The Nature of Personality Change in Adulthood

It has already been suggested that changes occur in physical appearance, social life patterns, personal relationships, role perceptions, cognitive processes, emotionality, and self-evaluation. There are literally hundreds of investigations carried out with adult subjects which substantiate the phenomenon of personality change in adulthood; and which, if they were to be evaluated and ordered from a common perspective, could perhaps be reduced to a more or less coherent description of the nature of the changes from one age level to the next. Rather than attempt any such broad-scale summary, however, I will select a relatively narrow focus. The primary concern here is with certain intrapsychic processes that relate to motives and affect, and with certain aspects of the organization of personality. It is necessary, first, however, to identify some of the concepts upon which I have relied.

Ego Processes

Concepts that appear to be most meaningful in studying adult personality are now emerging from ego psychology. As represented in the work of Hartmann (1958), Hartmann, Kris, and Lowenstein (1946), Murray (1938), Rapaport (1959) and others, and especially in the work of Erikson

(1959) and White (1960), these concepts constitute important modifications of psychoanalytic theory. Attention is focused upon the "executive" processes of personality, those that mediate between impulses and external demands, and those which test reality. The emphasis is upon processes of adaptation and choice; the growth of competence in dealing with the environment; and upon mental processes such as reasoning and cognition.

In ego psychology the concept of mutuality is stressed—that is, there is a crucial and continual coordination between the individual and his human environment; and that human character is by nature social. "Thus it is not assumed that societal norms are grafted upon the genetically asocial individual by 'disciplines' and 'socialization,' but that the society into which the individual is born makes him its member by influencing the manner in which he solves the tasks posed by each phase of his epigenetic development" (Rapaport, 1959).

The ego is seen as having a source of energy independent from the instinctual drives; and as following its own development through maturation and through continuous learning from interaction with the environment.

Personality growth is usually described in terms of a sequence of phases based on psychosexual maturation, in which each phase is characterized by a specific developmental task which must be solved by the ego. White (1960) has postulated, however, in addition to a model of psychosexual development, a model in which the individual strives to establish competence in dealing with the environment. He describes a set of motives which have their satisfaction in the individual's feelings of efficacy—what he calls "effectance motivation."

Ego Development in Adulthood

The ego is perceived as developing through a cycle of normative crises, each of which involves a re-ordering and rearrangement of feelings and preoccupations; and each of which, when mastered, results in a restructuring of the ego.

Although there have been various stage theories set forth by psychoanalysts and by ego psychologists, Erikson (1959), unlike the others, has delineated eight stages of ego development, three of which are specific to adulthood. The first four are seen as occurring in infancy and childhood, and have to do with the formation of basic trust, autonomy, initiative, and a sense of industry. In adolescence the crisis relates to the formation of ego-identity, the sense of self, and the sense of confidence in the persistence of the self. This is, in other words, the problem of "Who am I?" that characterizes the adolescent.

The first of the adult crises (the sixth of the eight stages) relates to the establishment of intimacy. This is the ability to merge one's self with the self of another; and to share intimately with another, as usually in the heterosexual relationship that becomes stabilized in marriage. Intimacy need not always involve sexual intimacy, but it always involves a true and mutual psychological intimacy with another person.

The next stage of ego development Erikson refers to as generativity. This is primarily the preoccupation with establishing and guiding the next generation. It relates to a sense of investment in the products of one's own creation (usually one's children, but also investment in other forms of altruistic concern and creativity, such as in the products of one's work). It involves also an identification with the future, and in this sense, a transcendance of the self and of the present.

The last stage Erikson refers to as integrity. This relates to the view of one's life as meaningful and inevitable—"the acceptance of one's own and only life cycle, and of the people who have become significant to it, as something that had to be; and that, by necessity, permitted of no substitutions . . . " The lack of ego integrity is signified by despair; the fear of death; the feeling, conscious or unconscious, that death comes too soon because one needs a last desperate chance to make something different of one's life (Erikson, 1959).

These formulations, as well as the related concepts from ego psychology, do not lend themselves easily to empirical testing. They are valuable, however, not only because they constitute one of the few attempts at a developmental theory of adult personality, but also because they seem to provide a meaningful framework for the findings that have emerged from many isolated studies.

The Self

Another set of concepts that are of particular importance in my thinking relate to those processes of personality that psychologists have called the "self." If there is a general characteristic that probably differentiates adulthood from childhood, it is that a growing importance is attached to self-awareness and to the impact of the self upon the environment.

There is, of course, a large body of literature now growing up in which "self" is the central concept. There are both theoretical descriptions and empirical studies of the self concept, of the self-image, and of self-actualization. Although a substantial portion of the theoretical literature deals with changes in self-image and with the effects of therapy (Rogers, 1951; Maslow, 1943; Syngg and Combs, 1949), certain of the concepts lead directly to the hypotheses that self-awareness increases throughout adulthood (but especially, as will presently be seen, in the later part of life); that the self becomes increasingly more differentiated; and that the qualities related to the exercise of choice and to the manipulation of outcomes become increasingly salient in human behavior. "Self" is the term Grinker (1957) uses to refer to "a super-ordinate process which functions in integrating the subsystems, including the many identifications that constitute the ego, ego-ideal, and super-ego, and in organizing behavior into available social roles." The growth of the self is also the process that Diggory (1962) is describing: "... The individual comes to regard himself as the instrument, sine qua non, for achieving his goals."

Self-initiated behavior and self-controlled outcomes are particularly important in viewing the effects of personality upon career lines, upon achievement, and upon adjustment. It becomes increasingly inescapable that what counts, in adulthood, is not the level of a particular ability, but what the individual makes of that ability; and that it is not the social or even biological condition that meets the eye of the observer, but what the individual himself interprets that condition to be. How else, incidentally, are we to account for the persons who, as Reichard has recently described them (Reichard, Livson, and Petersen, 1962), are the "successful" agers—the persons who, in the face of the same biological and social changes that insult their peers, manage nevertheless to put such a different face upon themselves and upon the world?

Changes in Ego Processes

To summarize in advance of presenting the evidence, my view is, in general, that there are sets of personality processes, primarily intrapsychic in nature, which show developmental changes throughout the life span. As the individual moves from childhood and adolescence into adulthood, the role of the ego becomes increasingly salient in personality dynamics. By ego is meant those processes concerned with relating the self to the environment; with selection, regulation, and integration of behavior; with the growth of competence and mastery; with the control of outcomes; and with the growing awareness of the self as the instrument for achieving one's aims.

In the broadest and most sweeping terms, the development of the ego is, for the first two-thirds of the life span, outward toward the environment; for the last part of the life span, inward toward the self. To elaborate, in these impressionistic terms: it is as if the ego, in childhood, is focused upon the development of physical, mental, and emotional tools with which to deal with both the inner and the outer worlds, and with which to carry on its transactions with the environment. In young adulthood, the thrust is toward the outer world, and toward mastery of the environment. In middle age, there comes a realignment and restructuring of ego processes; and, to the extent to which these processes become conscious, a re-examination of the self. In old age, there is a turning inward, a withdrawal of investment from the outer world, and a new preoccupation with the inner world. Finally, there is a stage in which the ego undergoes something of a last restructuring preparatory to death.

This is but a gross approximation of a developmental view of ego processes. It is, nevertheless, against this framework that I will elaborate certain concepts and sets of empirical findings.

Youth to Young Adulthood

The transition from adolescence into adulthood is, of course, a period marked by major transformation in the social personality, as the individual meets the major developmental tasks connected with vocational achievement, marital adjustment, home-making, and child-rearing. As already implied in the earlier discussion of continuity, however, findings are less clear with regard to changes in intrapsychic processes. In reviewing the literature on age changes in personality, it is interesting that there have been relatively few studies in which age-groups in the 20's and 30's are compared on the same measures with groups younger or older. (Even in the longitudinal studies referred to earlier, the results are usually reported in terms of change in relative position of individuals within the group, and not in terms of those characteristics that may be regarded as most salient in young adulthood.) With the growth of interest in gerontology, there are large numbers of studies now appearing in which young adults are compared with old; but even these studies are not directly relevant to our present purposes, for they have seldom been couched in terms of ego processes.

In any case, judging from descriptions of personality that emerge from a wide variety of studies, both experimental and observational, it is probably not too risky to generalize that development from adolescence to young adulthood is marked by an increase in expressivity, in expansiveness, and in extroversion. The high anxiety so frequently found in adolescents seems to decrease. Feelings of autonomy, of competence, and of stability increase. There is probably more equilibrium in mood, more integration of ego processes with impulse life, and relative stabilization of ego identity. A few of the studies which lead to these generalizations are those by Nawas (1961), Brožek (1955), Schaefer (1962), Willoughby (1937-38), Cattell (1957), Rongved (1961), and White (1952).

This is the tenor, for instance, of Sanford's conclusions, based upon studies of Vassar alumnae: "The evidence is that, in general, gains in the direction of greater complexity of personality, made in college, are maintained three to four years after graduation. But change does not usually continue after college. Instead, what seems to occur mainly is a kind of stabilization. When groups of young alumnae were retested with the use of a variety of personality tests three or four years after graduation, the only really significant differences lay in the greater stability, freedom from anxiety, and general psychological well-being shown in the later testing. . . . [We are] led to assume that there is a developmental phase, marked primarily by increasing stabilization of personality, that begins around the junior year in college and extends well into the alumnae years" (Sanford, 1962).

Young to Middle Adulthood

To continue at this level of generalization, it is probably safe to say that overt behavior and social personality seem to become even more stabilized in the period from young to middle adulthood. People move into a plateau in the middle years with regard to role performance; family, work, and recreational patterns show less change than at earlier or later periods in the life line. Self-reports, particularly those of middle-class and professional groups, tend to emphasize greater self-confidence, a sense of achievement and mastery, and an awareness of maturity. There is, for example, the well-known study by Strong (1931) of changes in interests of professional men aged 20-59, in which more change was found in the decade from 25-35 than in the two decades that followed. There is also the early study by Willoughby (1937-38), which indicates a drop in emotionality and mental stress by the 40's; there is the work of Cattell (1957), which shows a consistent increase in the direction of greater adjustment between ages 15-55; and there is at least one study (Neugarten and Peterson, 1957) in which the 40's are reported as the "prime" of life by middle-class respondents.

It is probably correct to conclude that with regard to intrapsychic processes, the period from young adulthood to middle adulthood is marked by a decrease in emotional reactivity, a decrease in tension, greater introversion, and a certain degree of "constriction" (probably a reflection of the greater preoccupation with the self that begins in middle adulthood).

Beginning in the period of the 40's, however, there seem to be the first signs of the major redirection of ego cathexis from outer to inner concerns.

In an early investigation of adult personality made within our group at Chicago, for example, three groups of men were studied, all of whom were employed in administrative positions in business (Schaw and Henry, 1956). One group had a mean age of 30; one, of 40; and one, of 50. In this study, responses to the Thematic Apperception Test were analyzed for dominant themes. The 30-year-olds were found to hold a view of the outer world as achievement-demanding. These men seemed willing to follow assertively the cues provided by the outer world; and seemed confident that one achieved one's goals by devotion to those demands and by relating directly and forcefully to an environment which is relatively uncomplicated. The 40-year-olds, however, saw the world in more complex terms. There was a re-examination of inner drives and a questioning of achievement demands, those demands which seemed so right and reasonable to the younger men. There was also an increased self-awareness and a preoccupation with one's emotions. The 50-year-olds seemed also to experience outer world events as complex; but they appeared to find resolution by moving to abstract integrative systems as means of dealing with the environment, and by preoccupying themselves with thought rather than with action.

The basic nature of the age change appeared to be a movement from an active, combative, outer-world orientation to the beginnings of an adaptive, conforming, and inner-world orientation.

(In the absence of other studies which bear directly upon this redirection of ego cathexis, there are those in which the findings are indirectly corroborative: the study by Willoughby (1937-38) which showed increased introversion in both sexes in their late 40's; a study by Gray (1947) which showed decreased extroversion through the middle-adult years; and a study by Hays (1952) which showed a significant trend toward constriction and introversion in Rorschach test performances beginning in the 50's.)

Middle to Old Age

There are several related studies of middle and old age which I wish to describe here. These are investigations, not all of them published, with which I have been intimately involved; and which, as a natural consequence, take certain priority in my thinking. There are, however, more objective reasons why they merit attention: as part of the larger set of inquiries known as the Kansas City Studies of Adult Life, they are all based upon large samples of normal people, and, with the exception of one group of very aged, upon samples drawn by probability techniques from the community at large. Furthermore, although they are cross-sectional studies, they have been designed specifically to clarify differences between age groups with regard to ego processes.

The overriding reason for describing these investigations in some detail, however, is that they provide what is, as yet, the best (although only partial) evidence for my thesis. By highlighting the transitions from middle to old age, you will notice that the usual procedure is being reversed—the procedure in which changes in the first part of life are used in drawing implications for later stages. In this instance, by focusing upon the last half of the life span, we shall be drawing certain implications with regard to the first half.

There have been, in the Kansas City studies, three different lines of investigation that bear upon personality. The first relates to the social personality, where attention has been focused upon gross patterns of social interaction and social competence, and upon behavior that is relatively overt and public. The second relates to personal adjustment and life satisfaction. The third is focused upon the more covert and less readily observed aspects of personality: the intrapsychic processes.

The inconsistent findings that have emerged in each of these three areas with regard to age differences are important in clarifying developmental changes in ego processes.

In the studies of social competence, there are neither significant nor consistent age changes from 40-65, but marked shifts thereafter. Thus, Havighurst (1957) rated the performance of 240 men and women from varying social class levels in the nine major roles of worker, parent, spouse, homemaker, user of leisure time, friend, citizen, club and association member, and church member; and found that the quality of role performance did not vary appreciably in the period from 40-65. It is not until individuals reached the mid-sixties, on the average, that gross patterns of social interaction showed marked changes. This is demonstrated also in studies by Cumming (Cumming and Henry, 1961), in which various measures of social interaction were utilized: the number of social roles, the number of hours of a typical day spent in interaction with others, and the total number of interactions with different kinds of people over an interval of one month. Here, with a sample of more than 200 persons aged 50-85, the most marked changes appeared around age 65.

With regard to adjustment and/or life satisfaction, our studies have shown no consistent relations with age. For instance, Peck and Berkowitz (1959) rated overall adjustment for a sample of 120 persons, 40-64 from all social class levels, and found no relationship to chronological age. Similarly, in a study (Neugarten, Havighurst, and Tobin, 1961) based upon four rounds of interviews taken over a period of two years with more than 200 persons, 50-85, ratings were made on five different components of life satisfaction (the individual's zest for life; his mood tone; his sense of resolution or fortitude; the congruence between his desired and achieved life goals; and the degree to which the self is positively regarded). There were no correlations with age. It appears, then, that age is not a significant variable with respect to adjustment, not only in the 25-year age span prior to 65, but probably in the decades of the 70's and 80's as well.[4]

---

4. This finding relative to life satisfaction in later years must be interpreted with great caution, since the age 70-80 subjects in these studies were individuals who suffered neither from major illness nor from economic deprivation, and thus constituted a relatively select group of survivors.

By contrast, when the investigations were concerned with issues such as the perception of the self vis-à-vis the external environment, the handling of impulse life, or the nature of ego boundaries, the findings led to the conclusion that there are significant and consistent age differences from 40 onward. These differences became clear when we moved to successively more covert measures of personality as, for example, from measures based upon interview data to measures based upon projective data analysed blind for age of respondent.[5]

The first of these projective studies was one based on responses of 131 men and women, 40-70, to a specially-drawn TAT-type picture (Neugarten and Gutmann, 1958). Although this study was primarily an investigation of perceptions of age-sex roles, the data suggested consistent age differences in personality. Forty-year-olds seemed to see themselves as possessing energy congruent with the opportunities perceived in the outer world; the environment was seen as rewarding boldness and risk-taking; and the individual obtained from the outer world what he put into it. For older respondents, the world was seen as complex and dangerous, no longer to be reformed in line with one's own wishes; and the individual was seen as conforming and accommodating to outer world demands. The protagonist was no longer a forceful manipulator of the object world, but a relatively passive object manipulated by the environment.

This study indicated also that with increasing age, ego functions are turned inward, as it were; and while rational thought processes are still important in the personality, thought becomes less relevant to action.

The same study suggested important differences between men and women as they age. For instance, men seem to become more receptive to their own affiliative, nurturant, and sensual promptings; while women

---

5. It may be of interest to educators, as well as to psychologists that there are special problems of research method involved in studies of adult, as compared to child, personality. Not only is the adult subject more practiced than the child in controlling the information revealed in an interview or on a test; but the investigator himself has difficulty in avoiding a shifting frame of reference in making evaluative judgments of performance in 40-year-olds as compared, say, to 70-year-olds. These problems are avoided to a considerable degree in studies based on projective test responses. Although the studies being reported here involve primarily the Thematic Apperception Test, inspection of other projective data on the same persons based on Sentence Completion and Draw-a-Person tests are corroborative of our overall findings with regard to age.

become more responsive toward, and less guilty about, their own aggressive, egocentric impulses.[6]

In another study (Gutmann, Henry, and Neugarten, 1959), the stories told by 144 men to four standard TAT cards were analyzed. The most frequent stories given by men in the 40-49 age group were those in which virility and resistance to coercion were stressed, and in which there was energetic and motoric approach to the environment. Intrusive energies were ascribed to the hero figures; passive and dependent wishes were denied; problems were thrashed out in combative interaction with the environment. Stories given by 50-year-olds were frequently those in which passive and deferent, rather than rebellious or defiant, heroes were projected. The stories of 50-year-olds frequently reflected conflict, in which short-range, sensual, and affiliative rewards were favored over long-range achievement goals; yet in which there was reluctance to retreat from the struggle with outer-world demands. In the stories given by 60-year-olds, these conflicts seemed to have been resolved. The most frequent stories were now those in which heroes were conforming, abasive, meek, friendly, mild, and in which aggression was perceived only in the external world. The stories were also those in which parental figures or impersonal institutional demands were important in the story outcomes.

A somewhat different approach was used in another study in which the hypothesis was tested that with increased age there is a decrease in energy available to the ego for responding to outer world events (Rosen and Neugarten, 1960). Four dimensions of ego function were measured from TAT data: the ability to integrate wide ranges of stimuli; the readiness to perceive or to deal with complicated or challenging situations;

---

6. Sex differences are consistent and often striking in studies of adult personality, just as they are in studies of child and adolescent personality. While the topic cannot be adequately treated within the limits of the present paper, there is considerable evidence that the sexes become increasingly divergent with age—perhaps, even, that we need two theories of adult personality, one for men and one for women. There is a study in progress at the Institute of Human Development, University of California, that deals with ego defense mechanisms and coping mechanisms in 40-year-olds (Haan, 1962) and in which a factor analysis shows differences in the structure of ego functioning between men and women. A factor which emerged for men, but not for women, was one with heavy loadings on intellectualization and intelligence as means of coping with impulse life. This is probably congruent with some of our findings from projective data, in which men, as they age, seem to cope with the environment in increasingly abstract and cognitive terms; women, in increasingly affective and expressive terms (Neugarten and Gutmann, 1958).

the tendency toward vigorous and assertive activity ascribed to story characters; and the tendency to perceive feelings and affects as they play a part in life situations. With a sample of 144 men and women, 40-71, divided into equal subgroups by age, sex, and social class, a three-way analysis of variance indicated that age was the significant factor in accounting for differences in the responses. Scores decreased regularly with age in the predicted direction.

Gutmann has investigated further the indication that concerns with inner life increase as aging progresses. Again working inductively from projective data (but drawing also, at later stages in the analysis, from other sets of data on the same individuals, including ratings and interview responses), he has formulated five personality types in men, 40-71, based upon these dimensions: 1) major concerns and preoccupations, especially in the area of impulse life; 2) the ego defenses or coping mechanisms elaborated in response to such preoccupations; and 3) the relative success or failure of these coping mechanisms. For women he also delineated five types, although the most salient psychological issues for women are not identical with those for men. For women, the dimensions underlying the typology include also the extent to which personal conflicts are externalized and projected onto the outside world; and the extent of intropunitiveness or extrapunitiveness. For both sexes, there was a consistent relationship between personality type and age, with a clear movement from active to passive to "magical" mastery approaches to the environment. Although the increased concern with self is projected in different ways by men and women, both sexes move to more egocentric, self-preoccupied positions, and attend more to the control or to the satisfaction of personal needs (Gutmann, 1961).

In summary, these studies demonstrated significant age differences in regard to intrapsychic aspects of personality. These differences refer primarily to the modes of relating to the environment and of dealing with impulse life. There is a change from active to passive modes of mastery, and a movement of energy away from an outer-world to an inner-world orientation.

That these processes begin to be measurable by the time persons reach their 40's is one point to be stressed, since in these years gross measures of social personality show no age changes.

The findings from these studies carried out in Chicago are generally congruent with the findings of other investigators, even though they have been formulated in somewhat different terms. Others have reported over and over again increased introversion in old age, decline in intellectual efficiency, and reduction in activities and interests. There are other findings described in terms of increased rigidity of personality,[7] stereotypy, flattened affect, conservation of energy, avoidance of stimuli, and what some investigators choose to call "regression."

Some of these findings, I submit, might better have been viewed as evidence of redirection, rather than diminution, of emotional investments; of change, rather than of decline. In general, however, no quarrel is intended with the view that, with advanced age, there is shrinkage in psychological as well as in social life space for most, although not for all, individuals.

At the same time, in describing the direction of change from outer- to inner-world preoccupation, I am not describing a change from expansion to restriction, as this process has often been described by others (Kuhlen, 1959). The latter may, indeed, be an accurate description of personality change in the adult years as, for instance, physical energy declines and as losses occur in many of those biological functions that are usually regarded as operating in the service of the ego—visual and aural acuity, memory, and speed of reaction time, to mention only a few. The expansion-restriction interpretation is usually presented, however, in terms somewhat different from my own—that is, as reactions to gains in early maturity, and as reactions to losses in old age. It is primarily with the concept of personality as a reactive set of processes that the present formulation differs.

The findings just described can, indeed, be interpreted differently: for instance, that as the individual ages he suffers sensory deprivation— or, more accurately, perhaps, both sensory and social deprivation; and that the response is "depressive" in reaction to the losses. Whether or not the change in personality has inherent as well as reactive qualities cannot yet be established, given the findings presently available. The major reason for my belief that certain of these changes are primarily in-

---

7. In an extensive review of the literature by Chown (1959), however, the concept of rigidity as a personality trait seems to have been put to rest. She has marshalled evidence to show that there are many types and many components of rigidity; and that rigidity cannot be generalized from one situation to another.

herent, or developmental, is that they occur well before the "losses" or aging. In other words, the fact that the personality changes I have described appear by the mid-40's in a group of well-functioning adults seems to me to be congruent with a developmental, rather than with a reactive, view of personality.

Engagement-disengagement

The studies just described have contributed to the theory of disengagement put forward by Cumming and Henry (1961). The contribution consists, in brief, in suggesting a disengaging process which may be primarily intrinsic, and secondarily responsive, and which leads to a state of decreased interaction between the aging person and others in the social group to which he belongs. The psychological aspects of disengagement include a change in behavioral motivation, with possibly a lessened desire for approval and love, increased freedom of choice of life rewards, an increased tendency to select short-run gratifications, and finally, a withdrawal from intense emotional attachments to people and objects.[8]

On the hypothesis that psychological disengagement occurs in old age, the implication is that in youth and young adulthood, as the individual's network of social interaction becomes progressively more complex and more engrossing, there is an accompanying increase in psychological engagement with the world of persons and objects. In short, the ego becomes increasingly preoccupied with the external world up through middle age; engagement-disengagement has its corollary, if not its forerunner, in the direction and redirection of psychological cathexis from external to internal stimuli.

Perceptions of Time and of Death

It will be noted that I am calling attention to the middle years of life —probably the decade of the 50's for most persons, although for some, it may come earlier—as an important turning-point in personality organization. Schilder (1940) undoubtedly had a similar point in mind when he

---

8. The theory of disengagement as set forth in the book Growing Old (Cumming and Henry, 1961) is being analyzed further in the light of new sets of data. Although all these data are not yet processed, it is likely that the theory will not only be elaborated, but also modified in major ways.

spoke of the phase of "libidinous rearrangement" as the first phase in aging.

In my view, this change occurs somewhat later than Erikson's generativity crisis in ego development. Although Erikson has not attached specific chronological ages to his stages of adult personality, the concept of generativity is centered upon involvement with children and upon the sense that one has contributed to the future. This fact leads me to believe that the restructuring of the ego in terms of generativity is one that must occur, for most persons, before they reach the empty nest stage in the family cycle.

Erikson's intimacy and generativity are both stages in which the ego is focused upon objects outside the self; they are both encompassed, accordingly, within that longer time period when the ego's primary preoccupation is with the outer world.

One of the processes that occurs in the middle years of life which promotes change in personality is the re-evaluation of time and the formulation of new perceptions of time and of death. Others have described these processes (Cumming and Henry, 1960) in somewhat different words; but whatever are the most appropriate terms to describe it, there comes a point, usually in the middle years, when the individual realizes that time is not infinite, and that the self will die. Along with this realization may come, also, an end to measuring one's life-time from the date of one's birth, and measuring it, instead, from the distance from one's death. This is the period when "the chips are down"—when one begins to take stock of one's life and to ponder what one may yet accomplish (or what one may yet obtain) in the time remaining.

Time takes on a new saliency for a great many, if not all persons; to judge, at least, from anecdotal and self-report data. (So far as I know, this change in perception of time has not been submitted to more systematic investigation.) It is at this point in the life line that introspection increases and contemplation of one's inner thoughts becomes a characteristic form of mental life.

I do not mean to imply that the introspection of middle age is the same as the reminiscence of old age; but it is its forerunner. It is probably a preparatory step in the final restructuring of the ego that is the symbolic putting of one's house in order before one dies.

The hypothesis that personality change occurs at the very end of life should not be relegated entirely to the realm of speculation. Recent work by Kleemeier (1961) on changes in IQ performance demonstrates a factor which influences the rate of observed decline and which, within the period of old age, is related to the imminence of death rather than to the age of the individual.

Similarly, there is the work by Lieberman (1962) on Bender-Gestalt and Figure-Drawing tests. In a small group of aged persons measured repeatedly at four-week intervals, there seems to come a point in time for each individual when his drawings of the human figure and his ability to reproduce the geometric figures of the Bender test undergo dramatic and irreversible change. The timing of these changes seems related to the time of death, and seems to occur in the absence of other observable social or biological changes that might be acting as precipitating events.

Whether or not these changes in performance are symptoms that herald imminent biological collapse, they are psychological in nature. Both these studies indicate personality change in the same general direction I have been describing—a shift in ego-organization and a shift in the direction of cathexis.

There is also the work of Butler who, drawing upon his clinical observations of aged persons, postulates the universal occurrence of what he calls the "life review." This is a process in which the aged individual, perceiving his approaching death, uses reminiscence to review his life. There is a progressive return to consciousness of past experiences and unresolved conflicts, in which these experiences are surveyed and reintegrated. While the process can lead to destructive as well as to constructive outcomes, it represents personality change that is often profound.

Within the present framework, Butler's observations are of special interest because he believes the life review occurs irrespective of environmental conditions.

I am not suggesting that adult educators should be expected to deal with this phenomenon of the life review. But if indeed it occurs in most persons, it is but another manifestation of the ego processes I have been describing; and it implies that the ego undergoes a final restructuring in preparing for death—if you will, another evidence of personality change that is developmental.

To restate: as is true in childhood and adolescence, changes in personality occur throughout the long period of life we call adulthood. Although the evidence is inadequate, there are data to support the position that changes occur in intrapsychic processes as well as in more readily observable behavior; such changes are orderly and developmental in nature; there is a general direction of change from active to passive modes of relating to the environment; there is a general movement of energy from an outer-world to an inner-world orientation; and the realignment and redirection of ego processes begins in middle age.

Thus, while it is not true that life begins at 40, it seems indeed to be true that life is different after 40.

References

Anderson, J. E. Prediction of adjustment over time. In I. Iscoe & H. A. Stevenson (eds.), Personality Development in Children. Austin: Univer. of Texas Pr., 1960. 28-72.

Brožek, J. Personality changes with age. J. Geront., 1955, 10, 194-206.

Butler, R. N. The life review: an interpretation of reminiscence in the aged. Psychiatry, 1963, 26, 65-76.

Cattell, R. B. Personality and Motivation Structure and Measurement. New York: World, 1957.

Chown, Sheila M. Rigidity—a flexible concept. Psychol. Bull., 1959, 56, 195-223.

Cumming, Elaine, and Henry, W. E. Growing Old. New York: Basic Books, 1961.

Davis, A., and Dollard, J. Children of Bondage. Washington, D.C.: Amer. Council on Educ., 1940.

Diggory, J. C. Death and self-esteem. Paper read at Amer. Psychol. Ass., St. Louis, August, 1962.

Erikson, E. H. Identity and the life cycle: selected papers. Psychol. Issues, 1959, Monograph No. 1.

Gray, H. Psychological types and changes with age. J. Clin. Psychol., 1947, 3, 273-77.

Grinker, R. R. On identification. Int. J. Psychoanal., 1957, 38, 1-12.

Gutmann, D. L. Personality in middle and later life: a Thematic Apperception Test study. (Unpublished paper on file with the Committee on Human Development, University of Chicago, 1961.)

Gutmann, D. L., Henry, W. E., and Neugarten, Bernice L. Personality development in middle aged men. Paper read at Amer. Psychol. Ass., Cincinnati, September, 1959.

Haan, Norma. Oakland Growth Study—progress report on ego mechanisms, defense and coping. Berkeley: Inst. of Hum. Devel., Univer. of California, 1961. (mimeographed)

Hartmann, H. Ego Psychology and the Problem of Adaptation. New York: Int. Universities Pr., 1958.

Hartmann, H., Kris, E., and Lowenstein, R. M. Comments on the formation of psychic structure. Psychoanalytic Study of the Child, 1946, 2, 11-38.

Havighurst, R. J. Social competence of middle-aged people. Genet. Psychol. Monogr., 1957, 56, 297-375.

Havighurst, R. J., Bowman, P. H., Liddle, G. P., Matthews, C. V., and Pierce, J. V. Growing Up in River City. New York: Wiley, 1962.

Hays, W. Age and sex differences on the Rorschach Experience Balance. J. Abnorm. Soc. Psychol., 1952, 47, 390-93.

Henry, W. E., and Cumming, Elaine. Personality development in adulthood and old age. J. Proj. Techn., 1959, 23, 383-90.

Hess, R. D. High school antecedents of young adult performance. Paper read at Amer. Educ. Res. Ass., Atlantic City, February, 1962.

Jones, H. E., Macfarlane, Jean W., and Eichorn, Dorothy H. Progress report on growth studies at the University of California. Vit. Hum., 1960, 3, 17-31.

Kagan, J., and Moss, H. A. Birth to Maturity. New York: Wiley, 1962.

Kelly, E. L. Consistency of the adult personality. Amer. Psychologist, 1955, 10, 659-81.

Kleemeier, R. W. Intellectual changes in the senium, or death and the IQ. Paper read at Amer. Psychol. Ass., St. Louis, September, 1961.

Kuhlen, R. G. A developmental psychology of adult life. In Developmental Theories of Aging. Princeton: N.J. Bur. Res. Neurol. and Psychiatr., 1959 (processed), 50-61.

Lieberman, M. A. Personal communication. August, 1962.

Maslow, A. H. A theory of human motivation. Psychol. Rev., 1943, 50, 370-96.

Mulvey, Mary C. Psychological and sociological factors in the prediction of career patterns of women. (Unpublished doctoral dissertation, Harvard University, 1961.)

Murray, H. A., and others. Explorations of Personality. New York: Oxford Univer. Pr., 1938.

Mussen, P. Some antecedents and consequents of masculine sex typing in adolescent boys. Psychol. Monogr., 1961, 75, No. 2 (Whole No. 506).

Nawas, M. M. Longitudinal study of the changes in ego sufficiency and complexity from adolescence to young adulthood as reflected in the TAT. (Unpublished doctoral dissertation, Univer. of Chicago, 1961.)

Neugarten, Bernice L., and Gutmann, D. L. Age-sex roles and personality in middle age: a thematic apperception study. Psychol. Monogr., 1958, 72, No. 17 (Whole No. 470).

Neugarten, Bernice L., Havighurst, R. J., and Tobin, S. S. The measurement of life satisfaction. J. Geront., 1961, 16, 134-43.

Neugarten, Bernice L., and Peterson, W. A. Study of the American age-grade system. Proc. Fourth Congr. Int. Ass. Geront., Merano, It., July 14-19, 1957. Vol. 3, 497-502.

Peck, R. F., and Berkowitz, H. Personality and adjustment in middle age. (Unpublished manuscript on file with the Committee on Human Development, Univer. of Chicago, 1959.)

Rapaport, D. Historical survey of psychoanalytic ego psychology. Psychol. Issues, 1959, Monograph No. 1. 5-17.

Reichard, Suzanne, Livson, Florine, and Petersen, P. G. Aging and Personality. New York: Wiley, 1962.

Rogers, C. R. Client-Centered Therapy. Boston: Houghton-Mifflin, 1951.

Rohrer, J. H., and Edmonson, M. S. (eds.). The Eighth Generation. New York: Harper, 1960.

Rongved, M. Sex and age differences in self perception. Vit. Hum., 1961, 4, 148-58.

Rosen, Jacqueline L., and Neugarten, Bernice L. Ego functions in the middle and later years: a thematic apperception study of normal adults. J. Geront., 1960, 15, 62-67.

Sanford, N. (ed.). The American College: A New Psychological and Social Interpretation of Higher Learning. New York: Wiley, 1962.

Schaw, L. C., and Henry, W. E. A method for the comparison of groups: a study in thematic apperception. Genet. Psychol. Monogr., 1956, 54, 207-53.

Schaefer, Judith B. Stability and change in thematic apperception test response from adolescence to adulthood. (Unpublished doctoral dissertation, Univer. of Chicago, 1962.)

Schilder, P. Psychiatric aspects of old age and aging. Amer. J. Orthopsychiat., 1940, 10, 62-69.

Snygg, D., and Combs, A. W. *Individual Behavior*. New York: Harper, 1949.

Strong, E. K., Jr. *Change of Interests with Age*. Stanford, Calif.: Stanford Univer. Pr., 1931.

Symonds, P. M. *From Adolescent to Adult*. New York: Columbia Univer. Pr., 1961.

Terman, L. M., and Oden, M. H. *The Gifted Group at Mid-life*. Stanford, Calif.: Stanford Univer. Pr., 1959.

Tuddenham, R. D. Constancy of personality ratings over two decades. *Genet. Psychol. Monogr.*, 1959, 60, 3-29.

White, R. W. Competence and the psychosexual stages of development. In M. R. Jones (ed.), *Nebraska Symposium on Motivation: 1960*. Lincoln: Univer. of Nebraska Pr., 1960. 97-143.

White, R. W. *Lives in Progress*. New York: Dryden, 1952.

Willoughby, R. R. The relationship to emotionality of age, sex, and conjugal condition. *Amer. J. Soc.*, 1937-38, 43, 920-31.

IV

MOTIVATIONAL CHANGES DURING THE ADULT YEARS

Raymond G. Kuhlen
Syracuse University

Whatever the specific role assigned to motivation by psychologists interested in learning and performance, there is little disagreement that it is an important variable, especially in the more complex types of learning and "real life" situations with which adult education is concerned. The psychological needs of individuals determine in part those aspects of the environment to which they attend and respond, the direction in which efforts are expended, and the amount of energy thrown into a task. But in addition, motivational concepts have proved extremely useful in understanding the behavior of individuals and groups at any one point in time; they are among the more important variables determining the course of development.

After consideration of some of the circumstances that result in developmental changes in motivation, the bulk of the present discussion will focus, first, upon growth-expansion motives, and second, upon anxiety and threat as a source of motivation. As one views the course of human life, growth-expansion motives seem to dominate the first half of the adult years, with needs stemming from insecurity and threat becoming important in the later years. While this is obviously an oversimplification, and circumstances will vary greatly among individuals and groups, these contrasting trends emerge from various studies of the adult life span.

Factors Influencing Developmental Changes
in Adult Motivation

At the outset, it may be worthwhile to examine some of the factors that are likely to result in important differences between people of various ages in their motivational patterns. Whether a need is aroused and influential, or quiescent and latent in particular phases of adult life will likely be a function of a number of the variables to be discussed below.

Changes in Arousal Cues, Environmental Stimulation, and Expectations

It is a matter of common observation, as well as a conclusion from psychological research, that even relatively satiated human desires can be aroused given the proper environmental stimulation, that motives may be weakened to the point of near disappearance after years of little opportunity for gratification or reenforcement, and that new motivational tendencies may appear if new types of stimulation or expectation (and reenforcement) are encountered. A society or culture decrees in many subtle ways, and in some not so subtle, that certain types of stimulation will be brought to bear on certain age groups and largely withheld from those of other ages. One of the problems that has plagued investigators of adult learning, for example, is the fact that once the adult has mastered his job, he is neither stimulated nor required to master new skills or understandings. The sameness of stimulation—whether on the job, in recreation, in marriage and sex—may be an important factor in the apparent decline of certain motivational tendencies, such as curiosity. An important, though unanswered, question concerns the nature of age trends under circumstances which permit or require that older individuals be subjected to new types of stimulation. Does a middle-aged person who changes jobs or spouses find career or sex drives rekindled, for example?

Moreover, since the motivational tendencies of people are very largely learned as a result of the reward and punishment systems to which they are exposed during the course of early development, it is reasonable to expect that motives may be <u>changed</u> during adulthood if the individual is exposed to a new set of punishment and reward patterns. Thus as an individual moves into a new role, e.g., is perceived by others as being middle-aged or old, he may be subjected to a new pattern of expectations, a new set of approvals and disapprovals, with the result that in due course new motives may appear.

Satisfaction of Needs and Changing Motivation

It is helpful in understanding some of the motivational changes that occur during the adult years to assume that human beings have a number of needs which vary in importance. In a sense, they are arranged in a hierarchy with the influence of higher level needs being to a considerable extent dependent upon the state of affairs with respect to lower level needs. Maslow (1943), among others, has argued that more basic needs must be satisfied before higher level needs become operative. This particular conception of the relationship among psychological needs is useful in explaining some of the changes in motivation that come with adult years.

Among middle-class Americans, for example, career drives are likely to take precedence over many other psychological needs, and dominate the years of young adulthood, perhaps even to the point of resulting in minimal contact with family. If by 40 or 45, the career-oriented individual has achieved economic security and success, the need to get ahead (the achievement need) may be much less in evidence, and the former career-oriented individual may more frequently turn to his family or to community activities as sources of gratification. Affiliation or service needs then may be more important. A similar change in the importance of sex as a drive may occur with the passage of years, and in part for the same reasons. In addition to having a strong sex drive in sheer biological terms, the adolescent or young adult is likely to be frustrated in his free expression and satisfaction of this drive. With marriage and more ready satisfaction of sex needs other motivations may emerge as important. One may speculate that Maslow's conception may partially account for the fact that sex needs may take precedence over convention in adolescence, whereas the reverse may be true of the parents of adolescents.

In sum, needs that are important in one phase of life may fade out and give way to others simply because they have become relatively satisfied. However, if circumstances should again arise which result in the frustration of a need previously satisfied, that need may again become active. For example, autonomy needs may be strong in youth, but become submerged as the individual becomes independent and self-directing. But if a situation should later arise where his autonomy is threatened, by a domineering employer or even by the protective cloak of kindness with which we sometimes envelop old people, then the need to be self-directive and independent may reassert itself.

Age-Related Frustration of Needs

It was suggested above that lower level or more basic needs may become inoperative and thus give way to higher level needs when they are satisfied. It is also not unlikely that chronic frustration will tend similarly to make a need inoperative. Lewin and his students pointed out some years ago that when children were unable to obtain an attractive goal object, such as toys within their vision but out of reach, they soon behaved as though the toys were no longer a part of their psychological field. Similarly, long and chronic frustration of some need may result in the individual's turning to other sources of satisfaction. His behavior seems subsequently to reflect other motivations. Thus, while a person may experience a reduction in achievement need and career drive because he has been successful, by like token he may experience a similar decrease because he has been chronically unsuccessful.

Because frustration may play a pervasive role in motivational changes, it may be worthwhile to specify some of the age-related factors that may prove frustrating and hence influence the motivational complex of the adult. Five sources of frustration merit comment.

First is the degree of status accorded people of different ages in the particular society in which they live. There seems to be general agreement that the American society tends to be geared to and to idealize youth, with the result that older individuals not only are frustrated somewhat with respect to status needs, but are very likely to encounter reduced opportunities for gratification of other important needs.

In the second place, people of different ages are likely to experience limitations and pressures of time and money. Man is a time-bound organism, in the sense that he has only 24 hours a day at his disposal.[1] This fact forces people, especially those in certain age ranges, to make choices among activities, to push aside certain interests and activities which they previously enjoyed. Unpracticed and unreinforced, often for many years, certain motivational tendencies may essentially disappear. As in the case of time, unavailability of money can result in certain needs dropping out of the picture, because of lack of practice and of reinforcement, whereas increasing availability of funds may result in their reappearance, and the development and cultivation of new needs.

Whereas time is relatively absolute and can be stretched only a little by efficiencies, money can be made to increase by appropriate expenditure of effort. Some data suggest that economic demands are greatest in the 30-40 decade (Johnson, 1951). Economic pressures, coupled and merged with career advancement desires, probably account for a large

---

1. Man also has a relatively finite life span. Time perspectives, in this sense, will be mentioned later.

share of the young adults enrolled in adult education programs. The force of the economic drive is apparent even in the history of geniuses whose productivity often bears a striking relationship to their need for money.

A third frustrating or limiting circumstance influencing motivation at different ages involves physical change and decline. The decline in physical energy, resiliency, strength, and reaction time—the general slowing down of the organism—has a pervasive effect upon behavior, perhaps as evident as anywhere in the recreational pursuits of people of different ages. While it is generally assumed that physiological drives are important motivators in infancy and early childhood, to be replaced gradually by the socially-derived motives which soon come to dominate the behavioral scene, the question may well be raised as to whether physiological pressures and tensions may not again become important motivators in the later years. One may argue that such would be the case; as frustrating agents they demand attention. In some cases there is general concern about and preoccupation with physiological functioning, but how general this may be is uncertain. And if physiological pressures again become important, they become so in a different psychological context. In early infancy social needs have not yet developed. In old age the difficulties of physiological function, of digestion and elimination, for example, and greater susceptibility to fatigue and illness may make satisfaction of derived needs more difficult or impossible and require greater attention to diet and general regimen. A re-emergence of physiological pressures as a motivating force may result.

Fourth, a middle-aged or older person may feel threatened and insecure because of skill deficits generated by rapid technological advance which have left him outdated. It should be noted that gains on vocabulary and information subtests of general ability tests may obscure this fact suggesting, as they do, increasing cognitive recourses as experience accumulates.

Fifth, and finally, is the greater threat and frustration that people may encounter because of their inability to do anything about some of the disturbing circumstances and sources of unhappiness which they experience. A person tends to get "locked in" particular circumstances as he marries, has children, invests in property, accumulates training and seniority, and may find himself unable to move out of a frustrating situation from which the younger uncommitted individual could easily free himself. Threats, such as loss of job, are thus much more serious for the committed and older individual than for the younger.

Critical Periods and Motivational Changes

The foregoing discussion has suggested that certain motives may be stronger at some periods of life than at others because of the degree to which special stimulation, special frustration, or satisfaction is encountered at those ages. Are there any particularly critical periods in the life span? Do, for example, changes such as those associated with the menopause result in a reorganization of the motivational structure of the individual? While the evidence is essentially negative with respect to the menopause period, it does seem probable that various factors combine to concentrate satisfactions and threats at particular periods of life. Scott and others (1951) have advanced the hypothesis that critical periods may be found at various points throughout the life span, particularly at those points when important changes in the social relationships of individuals occurred. If this hypothesis has merit, it may be expected that such events as marriage, becoming a parent or grandparent, or loss of spouse or job would influence in important ways the motivational pattern of an individual. Sometimes the effects may be dramatic, as in the instance of an elderly spinster who became quite a different person subsequent to the death of the domineering sister with whom she had lived her entire adult life.

Changing time perspectives represent another factor causing critical periods in motivational history. The point in life, perhaps the late 30's or early 40's, when one comes to the realization that time and life are not infinite, probably has quite a significant effect upon one's orientation and motivation. The here and now becomes much more important; if goals are to be achieved, they must be achieved soon. One is almost forced to structure his psychological present and future on a "real" rather than an "unreal" level. Biology and culture combine to set particular sublimits within the total span of life. Thus, 30 seems to be a critical time for the single woman hoping for marriage; the 40's for the individual striving for success in a career but not yet achieving it; the late 40's for the woman who has married late and wants children; retirement age for the professor who wants to finish a book before leaving the university.

Depending upon the circumstances in individual cases, critical points introduced by changing time perspectives may well result in reorientations of such magnitude that one can think of an important change in terms of goal object and motivational pattern. For others there may be a building up of unhappiness and anxiety, which in themselves represent strong motivating forces. And at any and all of these points there may be periods of serious self-appraisal.

Growth-Expansion Motives

In the introductory paragraphs to this paper it was pointed out that discussion would focus upon (a) growth-expansion motives and (b) anxiety and threat as a source of motivation. We turn to the first of these now, to an array of needs which can be considered together since they have in common the promotion of growth and expansion. These needs include those commonly assigned such labels as <u>achievement, power, creativity</u> and <u>self-actualization</u>, as well as broader orientation, suggested by such phrases as need to attain and maintain a significant role, need for expansion and ongoingness, and generative needs. Buhler (1951, 1957) who has written extensively on changing needs as major explanatory variables in the life cycle, tends to subsume such motives as just listed under the general category of <u>expansion</u>, and to urge that there is a continuing need for expansion throughout the life span. Though this is likely true, it is also probably true that such needs dominate behavior more obviously in the years up to middle age.

Achievement and Social Needs

A number of studies have demonstrated the greater importance of achievement needs in early adult years, especially for men (Kuhlen and Johnson, 1952; McClelland, 1953). A recent study by means of projective pictures of a nationwide sample of adults showed high points in young adulthood and middle age followed by a decrease in need achievement, but an increase in need power (Veroff, Atkinson, Feld, and Gurin, 1960).

In another study by Neugarten and Gutmann (1958) young men were described as actively striving toward goals, as self-propelled, achievement oriented. In contrast the older men were inactive, submissive, and introspective. Interestingly enough, while the female subjects did not give responses that could be categorized in the same way, they did portray the older female in the picture as characterized by a marked increase in dominance and assertion.

The data are not entirely consistent, however. Reissman (1953) for example, has reported that older high achievers were more willing than young high achievers to undergo the inconvenience of moving to a new city and to accept limitations upon freedom of religious and political expression for the sake of a better position.

Affiliation needs and social interests play a prominent role in life, and are here classified under growth and expansion needs; it is through expanding social relationships with individuals and groups that many people are able to achieve a sense of significance. Although it is difficult to infer whether there are marked changes in strength of affiliation and related social needs with age (the data of Veroff, et al., 1960, suggest a decline in the case of women), certainly there are important shifts in ways in which such needs are satisfied. There is, as is well known, an upsurge of social interest during the course of adolescence and into the early twenties. But from that point on there seems to be less interest in extensive social interaction with large numbers of individuals, and a shift to a greater liking for closer relationships with fewer people. Studies by Strong (1943) and by Bendig (1960) are consistent with this observation.

Changes in Goals

The postulation of a need or set of needs for continuing growth and expansion serves to relate in a meaningful way the goals and interests of people of different ages. As Buhler points out, family and work constitute major avenues of expansion, until these no longer offer possibility of continued satisfaction, whereupon interests shift to other kinds of activity. This shift from one orientation to another as a result of continued frustration of the possibility of expanding along the lines of marriage and family on the part of single women is illustrated in a study by the present writer (Kuhlen and Johnson, 1952). The basic data are presented in Figure 1. When asked what they most wanted to be doing ten years hence, the vast majority of young single women gave marriage and family as a goal. This response dropped off rapidly by 30 or 35 and was succeeded by desire to get a new or better job, a shift not apparent among married women. Other studies suggest that this process of forced reorientation in major goals is likely to be accompanied by considerable stress. The increasing participation of married women in organizational activities at around 50 years of age, as shown in another study done at Syracuse

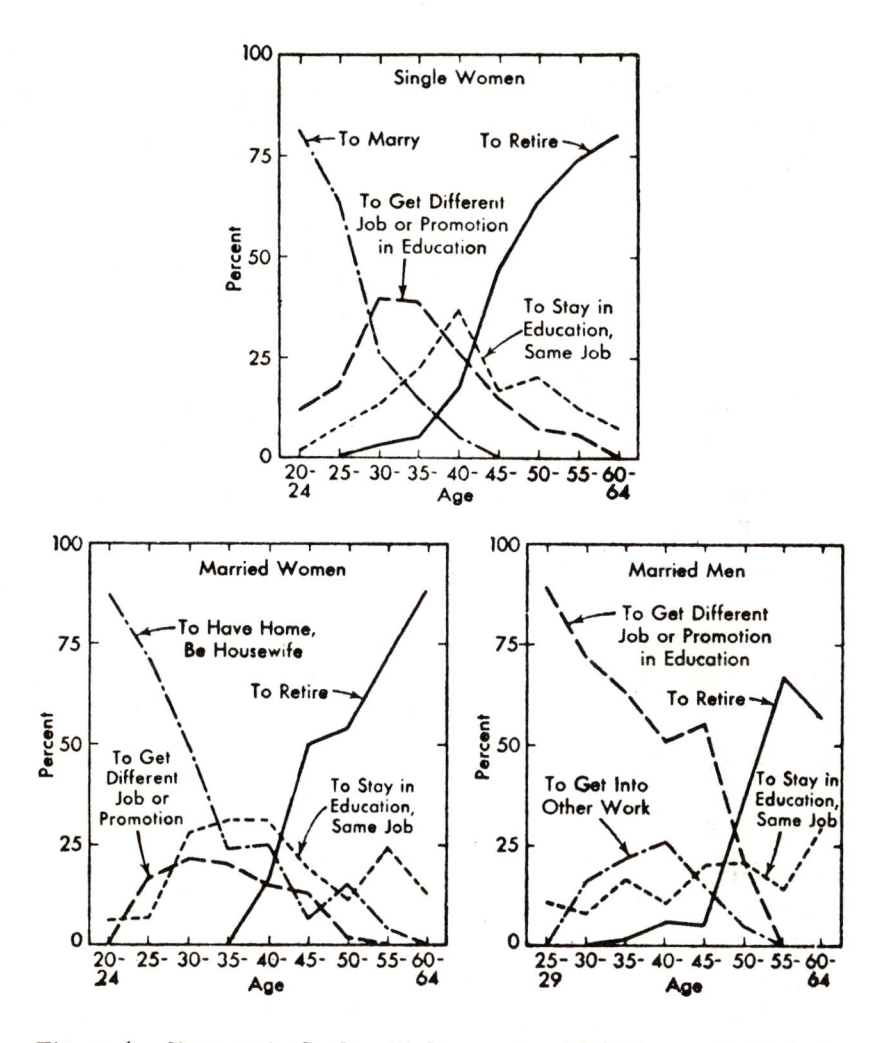

Figure 1. Changes in Goals with Increasing Adult Age as Reflected in the Responses of Public School Teachers to the Question, "What would you most like to be doing ten years from now?" (From R. G. Kuhlen and G. H. Johnson, Change in goals with increasing adult age, J. Consult. Psychol., 1952, 16:1-4. Reproduced with permission of the publisher, The American Psychological Association.)

(Kuhlen, 1951), may be interpreted as an effort to achieve a sense of significance in a new setting now that their children have left home.

An analysis of changes in interests, activities, and orientations with increasing years reveal a shift from active direct gratification of needs to gratifications obtained in a more indirect and vicarious fashion. An illustration of this trend is found in a study by the present writer (Kuhlen, 1948) in which an age in sequence appeared in reasons given for a major happy episode in life. Starting with the late teens or early twenties, the following sequence was evident: romance, marriage, birth of children, satisfaction with children's success. Presumably, through identification with one's own children, one achieves a sense of continuing expansion when one's own life becomes stagnant. It is of further interest, though not well documented in research, that older people evidence a greater interest in genealogy and in religion, and particularly in a belief in immortality. These orientations may well represent efforts, albeit unconscious, to maintain a sense of ongoingness even when it is recognized that one's own years are short.

Expansion, Constriction, and Degree of Investment in Life

Presumably, if Buhler is correct that needs for expansion are continuing, such shifts as just noted may reflect not so much a decrease in need strength (at least over a wide range of years) as a change in method of gratification necessitated by decreasing capacity or opportunity to obtain the gratifications as actively and directly as was possible at an earlier age. Figure 2 illustrates that life tends to be characterized by a curve of expansion and constriction. Constriction is forced upon the individual by extraneous circumstances. Retirement age is reached, spouse and friends die, opportunities are withdrawn. Also, the typical middle-aged or older person has less energy to invest, has fewer new experiences to relish, and has less reason to exert himself. For such reasons, he invests less in life.

This decreased investment in living with increasing age has already been suggested by the less direct methods of achieving gratification in later years. In total, there seems to be a reduction in drive level, a decrease in ego-involvement in life. The latter is reflected in analyses of Thematic Apperception Test stories obtained in the Kansas City study of middle and old age. Older people told less complex stories, introduced less conflict, and peopled their stories with fewer inhabitants. Also a reduction in ego energy seems to occur, as reflected in a count of the number of assertive rather than passive activities described and in ratings of the emotional intensity of the stories. The relevant data, reported in a paper by Rosen and Neugarten (1960), are summarized in Table 1.

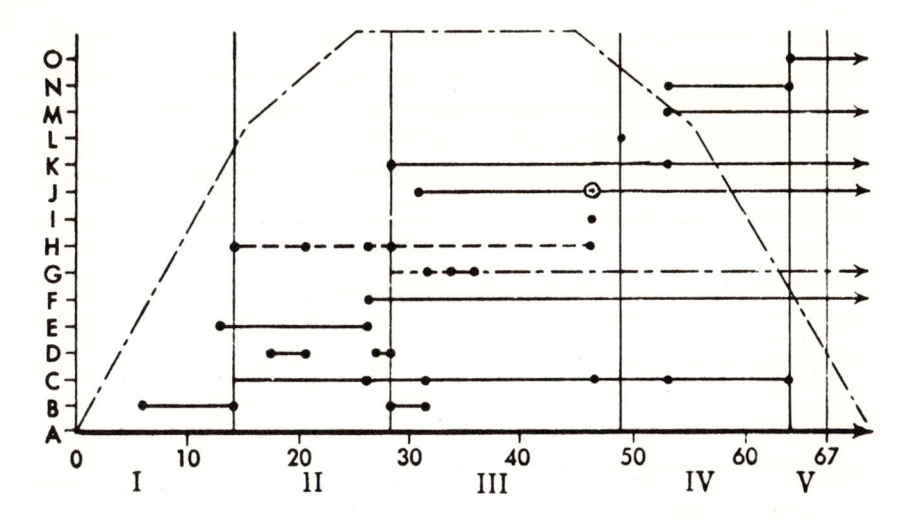

A. years
B. education
C. career
D. service in army
E. dating
F. marriage
G. children
H. change in domicile
I. extended trip
J. owns his own home
K. church and organizational membership
L. illness
M. children leave home and are on their own
N. operates own business
O. retirement

Figure 2. Schematic representation of Bill Robert's course of life. (From Buhler, Ch. Meaningful Living in the Mature Years, Chap. 12, pp. 345-87 in Kleemeier, R. W. (Ed.), Aging and Leisure, New York: Oxford University Press, 1961.)

Gurin et al. (1960) reported older people worry less than younger, a finding which they also interpret as reflecting less investment in life.

Paralleling the shifts described in Figure 2 for an individual, is a general pattern of expansion and restriction in a whole array of life activities. This is evident in age curves relating to income, family size, participation in organizations (Kuhlen, 1951), and in the social life space as reflected in the relative number of psychological settings penetrated in the community (Barker, 1961). Similar to these patterns are the curves obtained by Schaie (1959) for scores on a social responsibility test. These scores increased until the mid-fifties and then decreased among a sample of 500 subjects ranging in age from 20-70.

Table 1

Mean Ego-involvement and Ego Energy Scores of Men and Women Combined, Derived from TAT Data. (Adapted from Rosen and Neugarten, 1960)

Age	Number Interviewed	Ego-Involvement		Ego Energy	
		Introduced Figures	Introduced Conflict	Assertive	Emotional Intensity
40-49	48	2.23[a]	3.02[a]	13.19[a]	5.75
50-59	48	1.67[b]	2.38	12.27[b]	5.17[b]
64-71	48	.94[c]	2.35[c]	11.54[c]	4.08[c]

[a] Applying Turkey's test to the Studentized Range (Snedecor, 1956, pp. 251-52), the difference between means for the youngest and middle age groups is significant at or beyond the .05 level.

[b] The difference between means for the middle and oldest age groups is significant at or beyond the .05 level.

[c] The difference between means for the youngest and oldest age groups is significant at or beyond the .01 level.

Disengagement

Presumably data such as the foregoing, but more especially data from the Kansas City study of middle and old age, led to the recent proposal of a theory of aging to which was given the label "disengagement," an interpretation first presented in 1960 by Cumming and her associates, and later given more formal form and elaboration in a book (Cumming and Henry, 1961). This hypothesis asserts a reversal of a need for expansion, i.e., in later years the individual is motivated to disengagement. Though the point is not made as explicitly as might be wished, the implication is that the disengaged state of affairs is something <u>desired for its own sake</u> and not a second-best role adopted as a means of avoiding the threat developing in more significant participation, or as a result of societal rejection from more significant roles.

This theory has not been subjected to extensive tests, but some data are appearing. Thus a recent study bears on the hypothesis implied by those proposing the disengagement theory: in old age psychological equilibrium accompanies passivity whereas in youth active participation is necessary for equilibrium. The data recently reported by Tobin and Neugarten (1961) do not support this view. They found that an index of life satisfaction was correlated <u>more</u> highly with participation in older years than in middle age. Although the supporters of the disengagement theory hypothesize that there would be no loss in morale with increased age or with retirement, available data suggest such loss does occur. Kutner and his associates (1956) have shown morale to decrease with age, and Phillips (1957) has reported more maladjustment among old people. Another study, by Filer and O'Connell (1962), is especially noteworthy in that it involved an <u>experimental</u> manipulation of environmental conditions. A special attempt was made to modify the environmental demands and expectancies in a veterans' domicilary so as to provide a "useful-contribution" climate. Care was taken to avoid the appearance of a special project and the participants were probably not aware of the group they were in. Nor was the rater who evaluated their later adjustment. Significant gains in adjustment characterized the experimental group.

A recent report by Dean (1960), one of the collaborators in an early statement of the disengagement theory, has presented data on the decline of instrumentality in support of the theory. The present writer is inclined to place an opposite interpretation upon these findings, concluding that the data show oldsters to be quite unhappy about their lot because of their loss in instrumentality. The basic data in this study involved responses to the questions: "What are the best things about being the age you are now?" and "What are the worst things about being the age you are now?" The responses were classified in several ways, but we focus our attention here on two categories: (1) "<u>Output</u>: responses emphasize active engagement in the social environment, with focus on achievement, responsibility, power and influence, utility, knowledge, experience."
(2) "<u>Frustrated output</u>: The obverse of the above. Responses emphasize loss of ability to do, to achieve, to assume responsibility; loss of respect from others. This category includes responses about physical weakening, if this weakening is seen primarily as interfering with 'doing.'" It is significant that in response to the question concerning "best things" the output responses decline from 37% in the fifties to 3% in the eighties. This decline, in and of itself, does not indicate <u>purposeful</u> disengagement. Indeed, that people increasingly (with age) <u>resent</u> the loss of opportunity to achieve and assume responsibility is implied in the <u>increasing</u> frequency of responses to the "worst things" question, which fell in the frustrated output category. The percentages for four succes-

sive age groups (50's, 60's, 70's, 80's) were 22, 31, 53, and 48. In the two oldest age groups, 70-79, 80+, this response was the most frequent, suggesting real unhappiness at their inability to remain "engaged."[2]

One more example of inconsistency of data bearing on the disengagement hypothesis, that of religious interest, is appropriate inasmuch as there is no formalized pressure for a person to become disengaged from religious institutions as there is in the case of work. It will be recalled, also, that increased interest in religion in old age, particularly belief in immortality, was cited earlier as reflecting a need for continued expansion. Cumming and Henry (1961) are explicit on this point: "It is a common belief that religious piety and practice increase with age. . . . On the other hand, disengagement theory would predict a decrease in the interest in religion as normative control is lessened."

Not only do the data reported by these authors seem to this writer inconsistent within themselves, and inconsistent with their own hypothesis, but other studies have indicated an increasing belief in immortality throughout the adult years (Barron, 1961) with unanimous or near unanimous belief in the very aged groups, e.g., over ninety (Cavan, et al., 1949). Although extensive participation in church programs drops off with age, attendance holds up remarkably well in view of the general decline with age in out-of-home activities. Almost all evidence bearing on sedentary participation—radio listening, reading—shows an increasing interest in religion with age. Moreover, as Lehman (1953) has pointed out, more than any other organizations, religious organizations qualify as gerontocracies. It is not unlikely that the differences of opinion regarding the importance of religion in old age lies in that there are several possible indices of religiousness. Indices based on different definitions will show contrasting trends.

Despite the contradictory lines of evidence summarized in the foregoing paragraphs, it is probable that the disengagement concept will have considerable heuristic value. Already it appears to have stimulated a variety of studies which have added to the store of empirical data on aging, and it may well provide an appropriate explanation of aging trends in an as yet undefined segment of the population even though not applicable to the generality.

---

2. An older study by Simmons (1946), contradicts the disengagement hypothesis.

Anxiety and Threat as a Source of Motivation

We turn now to another source of motivation—anxiety—which as noted earlier increases and becomes more generalized as people move into the middle and later years. This anxiety may not only generate constructive efforts to reduce it, sometime through education or therapy, but is especially important in adult education as a generator of defensive and handicapping behavior patterns. It was suggested that there is reason to believe that social and physical losses, coupled with increasing responsibilities and commitments, may well generate increasing anxiety with age. It is probable that the tendency to become anxious and susceptible to threat bear an increasingly important motivating force during late middle-age and the older years. A number of writers (e.g., Kaufman, 1940; Atkin, 1940) who have attempted theoretical explanations of the aging process, have seized upon anxiety generated by social and physical losses as the primary age-related independent variable. Various personality changes, such as conservatism, intolerance of ambiguity, and rigidity are construed as ego defenses, or maneuvers, utilized to control the anxiety so generated.

It should come as no surprise that this particular interpretation of aging is not well accepted by middle-aged or aged people. When the writer presented these views at an adult education conference some years ago, it was denounced as "a theory of decay." While, to be sure, there is much that is virtuous in an emphasis upon positive achievement and "expansion," a realistic approach requires that we take into account the negative side of the motivational picture as well.

Anxiety is one among a number of symptoms of maladjustment. A recent factor analysis by Veroff, Feld, and Gurin (1962) of the symptoms of subjective adjustment and maladjustment has identified several dimensions that warrant our attention. Five factors were identified in the analysis of the data for males: (1) felt psychological disturbance, (2) unhappiness, (3) social inadequacy, (4) lack of identity, and (5) physical distress. All but the last were also apparent in the analysis for women.

Changes in Subjective Happiness

It is axiomatic that a person is not well adjusted unless he is reasonably happy and contented. About the only way one can discover this is to ask him. Subjective though the data are, they nonetheless have important implications for the issue at hand. Although the trends to be reported are for happiness, it seems reasonable to assume that the trends for unhappiness, which are more directly suggestive of anxiety, would be essentially the mirror image of the curves for happiness, though a neutral group (neither happy nor unhappy) might vary in size from age to age and thus make the reflection less than exact.

One would anticipate that happiness would increase with age as important previously-frustrated needs are satisfied. Thus in young adulthood, in contrast to adolescence, sex needs and needs for autonomy are more likely to be satisfied, and important life developments in family and work bring a sense of achievement and security, and presumably happiness. An unpublished study by Kuhlen (1948) shows this curvilinear relationship and studies by Morgan (1937), Landis (1942), Gurin and his associates (1960), and Caran and others (1949) show losses in middle and later years.

We have, then, in one important symptom of adjustment, an indication that as people get older, at least beyond middle age, their reported happiness decreases on the average and presumably the incidence of unhappiness increases.

Changes in Self-Concept

It is apparent that the well-adjusted individual will have positive self-regarding attitudes, whereas the individual who is maladjusted and insecure—and hence more susceptible to anxiety and threat—will tend to have low regard of himself and be lacking in self-confidence. Again, one would anticipate that the character of the self-concept would vary curvilinearly with age, becoming more favorable during the periods of gains and increased status, and less favorable in the years beyond. Although there have been interesting theoretical considerations of developmental change in self-concept during the adult years (see particularly Erikson, 1959, and Buhler, 1962), there are relatively few developmental data available. Lehner and Gunderson (1953) show a curvilinear relationship of self-concept to age utilizing the draw-a-person test. It was found that men tended to draw larger figures the older they got up to about age 30 and thereafter they draw smaller pictures, whereas women draw larger pictures up to age 40 and then smaller pictures. Since it is often assumed that in such picture-drawing the individual projects his self-image, it possibly may be inferred that these trends reflect self-evaluation, and that the picture is drawn larger until the individual senses that he has passed the prime of life.

Some of the data on self-concept in later years are on the amusing side, though nonetheless revealing. For example, when taking intelligence tests in the course of an experiment, older college professors made twice as many self-belittling comments as did those younger (Sward, 1945). And older women,[3] particularly older single women, have a strong tendency to omit their ages from autobiographical sketches in such places as Who's Who and American Men of Science (Norman, 1949). Presumably this is done because such admission is painful to themselves, or viewed as self-damaging in the eyes of others. More systematic is the study by Mason (1954) who administered a number of measures of self-concept to several groups from different backgrounds. A group of institutionalized indigent old people had more negative self-concepts than did a group of independent, middle-class oldsters, and both, in turn, had more negative self-concepts than did a more youthful, low economic group. However, individual differences among the aged groups were greater than among the young, suggesting that reactions to the aging process vary substantially among individuals.

How one classifies one's age may be construed as reflecting his self-concept. The surprising finding from several studies (Tuckman and Lorge, 1954; Phillips, 1957; Kutner, et al., 1956) is that many people of quite advanced years often describe themselves as "middle-aged"—half of over 300 individuals over 70 years of age in one of the studies and about a third of those over 75 in another. That one's subjective age has significant implications is suggested by the fact that, with actual age controlled, those oldsters who rated themselves as middle-aged in one study (Havighurst, 1953) were better adjusted on other measures, and that in another study (Kogan and Wallach, 1961) a relationship was found between subjective age and indices of caution, when chronological age was held constant. Curiously, however, this latter relationship was attributable almost entirely to a rather high relationship to subjective age and caution in that portion of the group that was low in measured anxiety. The investigators considered the lack of relationship between subjective age and "decision caution" in the high anxiety group to stem from the greater heterogeneity

---

3. Age, incidentally, was estimated by facts they gave regarding year of graduation from college.

of this group, a circumstance they thought due to the different possible meanings of high anxiety for older people. For the low anxiety subjects, the theoretical interpretation stressed the importance of "image maintenance" in bringing about behavioral consistency.

This relationship between self-concept or self-image and "decision confidence" brings us to another major line of evidence relating to self-concept, namely, that bearing on the self-confidence of individuals of different ages. As suggested above, one would expect that individuals with positive self-concepts would be more self-confident, whereas those with negative self-concepts would be less self-confident. Following our expectation that self-concept would improve during those phases of the life span where there are pronounced gains and evidences of accomplishment, Brozek (1952) has shown that men around 50 were more self-confident on a questionnaire than younger men. Wallach and Kogan (1961) compared younger adults (college age) with a group of older adults (between 47-85) on a number of measures of caution and self-confidence. They found a number of relationships including the fact that the older group was more cautious than the younger group, and, in the case of men, less self-confident. The basic facts are presented in Table 2 where it is also shown that a reliable relationship between caution and age exists among the older group of women, but not among the men. These data suggest that aging experiences in the American culture affect the sexes differentially with respect to decline of confidence and caution, both with respect to timing and degree.

Another, possibly very significant, finding was the fact that the odd-even reliability of the test involving degree of caution (a dozen verbally described situations with respect to which the subjects were asked to recommend action) was higher for the older group (r: males, .80; females, .80) than for the younger group (r: males, .53; females, .63). This finding may be interpreted as indicating a greater _generality_ of caution, i.e., less dependence upon specific situational factors, among the old than among the young. This particular finding, if confirmed, has substantial theoretical significance. The fruitfulness of a theoretical interpretation of aging in terms of anxiety and threat depends in part upon the degree to which anxiety is shown to be generalized and not highly situational in origin.

Another study (Kogan and Wallach, 1961) is of interest here because

Table 2

Age Differences in Self-Confidence and Caution.
(Adapted from Wallach and Kogan, 1961.)

	Young	Old	p	r* (older group)
Confidence Index (Low scores indicate confidence)				
Men	2.83	3.19	.01	–
Women	3.11	3.08	NS	–
p	.01	NS		
Deterrence of Failure (Caution) (High scores indicate caution)				
Men	5.82	6.38	.01	.05 (NS)
Women	5.88	6.36	.02	.33 (p .01)
p	NS	NS		

*Correlation is between age and "deterrence of failure" score and age in the older group. "Older men" averaged 70.2 years (SD± 7.3); women 69.5 years (SD± 7.7). Number of subjects: 132 young women, 89 older women; 225 younger men, 65 older men. Young people were college students.

it compared values placed upon different phases of the life span by a younger and an older group of subjects. With respect to "self-concept," the concepts "myself" and "ideal person" were included among those studied by means of the semantic differential, with special reference to the evaluative factor score. Here again a decline in the favorability of the self-concept in old age appeared. The difference between the old and young was especially significant in the case of the "ideal person." This was interpreted by the authors as suggesting "that older individuals are either more willing to admit unfavorable elements into their image of the ideal or that the very connotation of the concept evokes a more negative reaction in an older person whose age status renders unrealistic any aspirations toward an unrealized ideal self. . . . However, such devaluation may have ego defensive properties for both old and young individuals."

Table 3 contains scores on the evaluative factor for those concepts relating to developmental stages in life. Both young and old age groups of both sexes assign negative valuations to such concepts as elderly, old age, and death. However, the older individuals were reliably less negative toward old age and death than were the younger. Thus, while older people place a negative valuation upon their phase of life, they seem to

Table 3

Age Differences in Mean Evaluative Scores (semantic differential) for Several Life Stage Concepts. (Adapted from Kogan and Wallach, 1961.)

	\multicolumn{6}{c}{Concept}
	Baby	Youth	Middle Age	Elderly	Old Age	Death
Men						
Young	2.24	.99	.61	− .77	− .97	−3.02
Old	1.75	1.05	.29	− .69	− .11	−2.25
p	NS	NS	NS	NS	.02	NS
Women						
Young	2.32	1.17	.22	−1.02	−1.79	−4.28
Old	2.09	1.35	.20	−1.14	− .30	−2.33
p	NS	NS	NS	NS	.001	.001

achieve a certain adaptation to old age, and do not view it nearly as negatively as do young adults.

Changes in Incidence of Anxiety Symptoms

Evidence presented thus far in this section indicates rather clearly that as people get older, they are less happy, have more negative self-concepts, and have experienced a loss of self-confidence. One would expect increases in anxiety symptoms to parallel these changes. Trends should be examined under two conditions: first, under what might be considered normal circumstances of living, and second, under stressful or threatening conditions. Study in these two settings is desirable because, as is the case of physiological functioning, the effects of aging are not likely to be so noticeable under normal conditions as under conditions of stress. Thus, we might anticipate that people would not show anxiety symptoms with age under normal conditions of living, but would under conditions of environmental or organic stress.

The bulk of the data obtained under ordinary conditions of living seem to be consistent with this expectation. Despite the common expectation that nervousness would increase with age or be particularly noticeable at certain critical points, such as menopause, no particular age trends appear (Hamilton, 1942). Nor was an increase with age in the frequency of nervous symptoms evident among a large number of individuals taking health examinations in another study (Britten, 1931). No age trends or a trend toward decreased anxiety might well be expected, in view of the fact that people tend to seek out those circumstances in life which are positively rewarding and non-threatening. To the degree that one is successful in this, as he is likely to be as time (age) passes, and so long as this state of affairs is maintained, no increase with age in anxiety would be anticipated. This seems to be the finding of a number of early studies.

However, certain facts emanating from a recent national mental health survey are contrary to the earlier findings and warrant particular attention because of the size and representativeness of the sample. The interview schedule used in this survey contained questions dealing with 20 symptoms of psychological distress. A factor analysis suggested four factors which were labeled "psychological anxiety," "physical health," "immobilization," and "physical anxiety." Table 4 carries the percentage of subjects in various age groups who evidenced high scores on three of these factors. It will be noted that there is a substantially greater incidence of anxiety symptoms among older people than among younger except in the factor immobilization.

Table 4

Percentage of Subjects of Various Ages Who Received High Scores (6, 7 or 8) on "Psychological Anxiety," "Immobilization," and "Physical Anxiety." (Adapted from pages 190-92, Gurin, Veroff, and Feld, 1960.)

	Age					
	21-24	25-34	35-44	45-54	55-64	65+
Psychological Anxiety						
Men	5	6	8	11	14	17
Women	10	14	17	20	29	34
Immobilization						
Men	22	10	10	3	1	2
Women	14	15	12	6	5	4
Physical Anxiety						
Men	3	4	4	8	13	17
Women	8	9	10	14	17	28
No. of Subjects						
Men	65	252	241	209	146	161
Women	98	344	307	250	183	191

These investigators offer the following interpretation of the greater incidence among young adults of anxiety symptoms classified under the tentative label of immobilization:

> Immobilization, ennui, and lack of energy are all psychological states that suggest lack of integration, rather than insurmountable, immediate psychological difficulty. In a life situation, where one is caught among different pressures for integration of the self—pressures that may operate at cross-purposes (such as the "achievement versus housewife" conflict for some women) or pressures that are so varied that they are not all attainable at the same time—one may frequently experience a lack of integration. Such pressures are more likely to occur early in life and then gradually diminish as patterns of integration are chosen. Until such integration occurs, however, one might expect that a common reaction to these cross-pressures which are too divergent or too numerous to handle would be withdrawal, with its concomitant restlessness and disruption. Since this problem is more often encountered by the young adults, perhaps this is one reason that young people are prone to symptoms of the immobilization type (Gurin, Veroff, and Feld, 1960).

Adequate explanations of the contrast between this recent study and earlier findings are not readily apparent. Differences in methodology or in sample may be responsible, or it may be that current times are confused and stress filled compared to the social-political context of earlier research. As will be developed next, older individuals seem particularly susceptible to stress, and thus it is possible that under current "normal" conditions they may reflect more anxiety.

For more definitive evidence regarding reactions of people of different ages to stress situations, one may cite reports of observations in "naturalistic settings" and studies which were specifically designed to check this phenomenon. Welford (1951), among others, offers as one explanation of the reluctance of older individuals to cooperate in experiments, their unwillingness to expose themselves to the threat of the new situation. Another study of younger adult years (Kuhlen, 1951), done during World War II, revealed a greater relationship between age and anxiety symptoms among enlisted naval personnel who were presumably in a more tense situation than were others.

Two other studies, using different procedures, suggest an increase in anxiety with age. In these studies, reaction time to stimulus words was used as a measure of threat or stress. While data bearing on words representing different areas of life will be considered below, relevant to the current discussion is the reaction time to words such as worry, afraid, unhappy, restless, and anxious. Such words may be considered generalized anxiety "stimuli" in contrast to a word like "church" which represents the religious area of life. Powell and Ferraro (1960) in one study and Olsen and Elder (1958) in another found reaction time to these words to increase with adult age. Since these generalized anxiety words were interspersed with words from potentially stress filled areas of living, it is not clear whether the results should be construed as bearing on changes under "normal" circumstances of living or under "stress" circumstances.

Although the data are by no means as extensive as one might wish, either with respect to the range of symptoms sampled or the range of ages, the evidence does suggest that increasing age brings increasing susceptibility to stress and threat. Presumably this threat is engendered by cultural and physical losses that are experienced with increasing age, and by commitments which are more binding as age increases and which make threats more serious. Certainly more careful studies should be undertaken of this variable, not only for marking out the age relationships under different conditions, but also to determine the degree to which increasing age brings a generalized anxiety which might be reflected in an array of behaviors, in contrast to anxiety which is fairly specific to certain situational changes that occur with age. In view of the theoretical importance of anxiety as a variable influencing personality, and performance changes with age, such studies assume great importance.

Specific Sources of Anxiety as Related to Age

The foregoing discussion has given some indication of age changes in the gross anxiety present at different ages as this is reflected in general anxiety symptoms. Data indicating particular sources of worry and anxiety are likely to be useful to adult educators and others concerned with human betterment. Like the sequence of "developmental tasks" described by Havighurst (1953), they suggest both curricular content and timing.

That there can be striking age differences in the source of anxiety and tension during the young adult years and middle age is shown in the data presented in Figure 3. In this study, instead of using a verbal questionnaire, subjects were presented with words, taken one at a time, which were chosen to represent different areas of living. Since it is well known that people tend to block up, and thus to react more slowly to stimuli

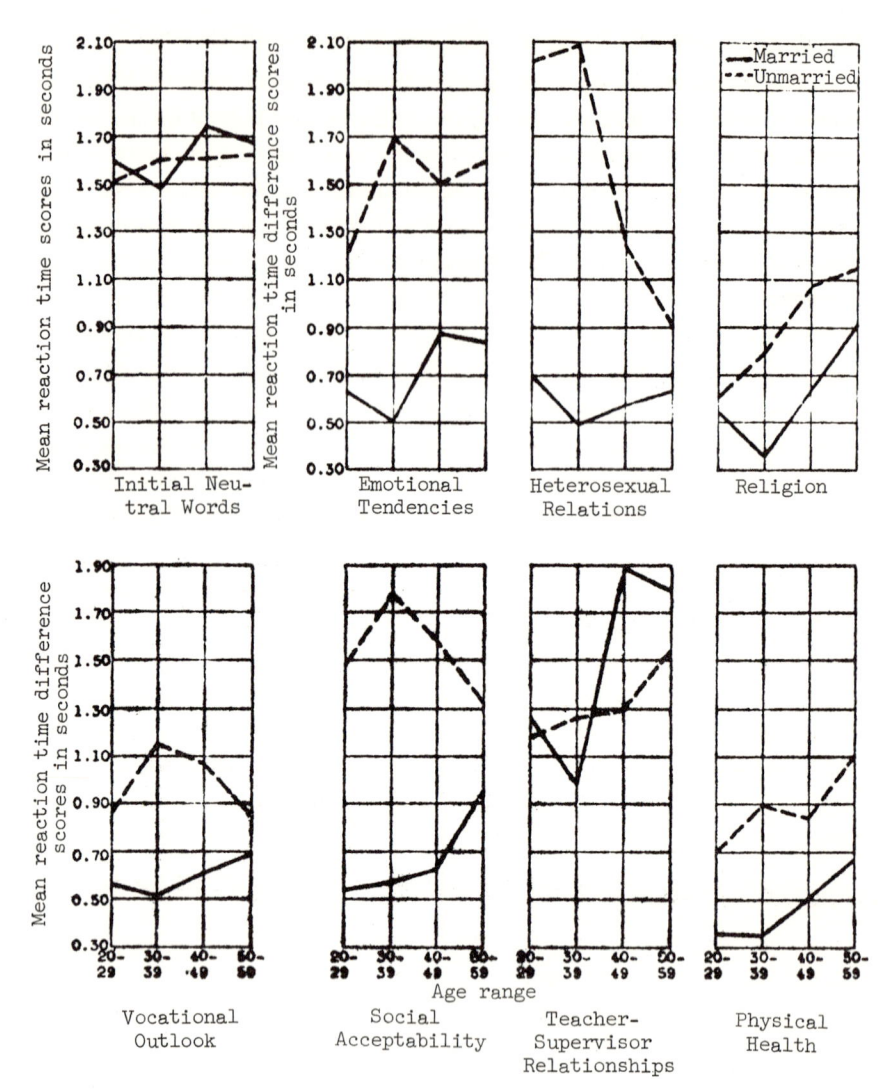

Figure 3. Mean reaction time scores in seconds of married and unmarried teachers at various age ranges to initial neutral words, and mean reaction time difference scores in seconds of married and unmarried teachers at various age ranges to "critical" words taken from various psychological adjustment areas. (From Powell and Ferraro, 1960, by permission of the publisher, The American Psychological Association.)

which are disturbing to them, comparison of their reactions to these critical words with their reactions to a list of neutral words can be taken as some indication of the degree to which particular areas of life sampled by the critical words represent sources of anxiety or tension.

The subjects in this study were all white female public school elementary teachers, half of whom were married and half of whom were single, 25 of each group in each of the age categories are shown in the chart. There are important differences between those who are married and single, i.e., between those who occupy different roles in life and hence are exposed to different threats and have different opportunities for need satisfaction. Particularly striking is the anxiety evoked by heterosexual words among single women in the younger adult years and the rapid drop-off as age increases to 60. Married women, who have greater potential for satisfaction of sex needs, show relatively little anxiety and relatively slight change with age. Single women, for whom career begins to become a primary source of satisfaction by around 30, show a peak of concern with this area in the 30's, whereas married women show little change with age. Similar striking differences are found between the married and unmarried groups with respect to social acceptability, but in the instance of religion, physical health, and teacher-supervisor relationships the trends are similar, increasing with age in each instance. It is of some significance, that in each of the seven areas, with the exception of teacher-supervisor relationships, single women show more anxiety and concern than do married women. Whether this is due to selection, the more maladjusted being those who do not marry, or due to a generalized anxiety resulting from a "minority group" status is not clear.

Other data (Dykman, Heiman, and Kerr, 1952) confirm the fact that different ages in young adulthood and middle age are characterized by different problems, and suggest that changes in problems continue into old age. Morgan (1937) and Havighurst and Albrecht (1953), among others, have presented data describing specific worries of very old people.

Individual Differences

It has been argued in this paper that the changing motivational picture of the adult years can be painted in two broad strokes, one emphasizing growth-expansion motives which are translated into a succession of goals, the other emphasizing anxiety, generated by physical and social losses, which constitute the motivational source for handicapping, but nonetheless protective, defense maneuvers. Although both motivational patterns are important throughout life, the first more clearly dominates the young adult years, the latter the later years of life. Whatever merit such a conceptualization may have as far as the generality is concerned, it is obvious that there will be important differences among individuals as to how and the degree to which these tendencies are translated into specific goals or defensive maneuvers, and the ages at which one tends to outweigh the other. As illustrative of differences among individuals, it is instructive to examine contrasts between meaningful subgroups of the population where data are available.

Differences in the Onset of the Threat of Age

It may be hypothesized that a critical point, motivationally, in the life history of the individual is that point at which he senses that the process of expansion is concluding, and becomes sensitive to certain irreversible losses. Such a point would presumably be somewhat delayed in oriental culture where age is venerated, as compared to western culture where an unfriendly attitude toward old age is probably more characteristic. Generally speaking, in those subcultures (or in those individuals) where age brings continuing success and status, there presumably would be less threat associated with the process than in a subculture (or in an individual) where losses are experienced relatively early.

While data are not available for all subcultures, the point can be made by selected sample data. Incidence of suicide varies greatly between the sexes and between Negro and white groups. Whereas the rate constantly climbs for white males with age, for females it is a relatively level smoothly rounded curve, with an actual decline in the advanced years. These differences may be interpreted as reflecting more stress in the environment in which males live, and the fact that with increasing age it is more difficult for them to maintain their role. Geared as men are to the work life, career frustrations and inability to find useful employment presumably would be a serious blow to self-concept and the generator of unhappiness and anxiety.

Two lines of evidence are presented with respect to social economic and social class differences. The first involves social class differences in the way people perceive the prime of life and aging. In Table 5 which summarizes answers given by men and women, the most striking difference relates to answers to the question of when is a man "mature," "at the prime of life," "most confident." The lower-lower class individuals gave 25 years of age and those in successively higher social classes reg-

Table 5

Differences among Social Class Groups in Their Perception of Aging (From p. 4a of Aging and the Aged, <u>The University of Chicago Reports</u>, Vol. 12, No. 2, November 1961)

	Upper Middle	Lower Middle	Upper Lower	Lower Lower
Men Look at Aging When is a man...? "Mature," "at the prime of life," "most confident" "Middle-aged" "Old"	40 47 70	35 45 70	30 40 60	25 40 60
Women Look at Aging When is a woman...? "Good looking" "Most confident" "In her prime" "Old"	35 38 40 70	30 35 40 70	27 30 38 67	25 35 35 65

ularly raised the age until those in the upper middle class gave a mean age of 40. Similarly upper middle class individuals defined "middle age" and "old" as notably older than did those in lower-lower class groups. When women were asked what age a women was most "good looking," "most confident," "in her prime," or "old," again the lower-lower class groups gave lower ages than did those in the upper-middle classes.

But perhaps more critical than such perceptions is the age at which economic threat is experienced by members of different occupational categories. We go back to 1940 for the best example of this phenomenon, since it would be under conditions of economic stress that such threats would be most clearly revealed. The data in Figure 4 show clearly that it is the laboring group which experiences earliest and in most pronounced fashion the threat of loss of employment. In the upper professional group, very little change occurred with age. These people, even under strained economic conditions, seemed not particularly threatened by loss of employment regardless of age.

Other significant subgroups of the population can very readily be identified. Buhler (1933), for example, has contrasted a "psychological curve" of life with the "biological" curve of life, and has pointed out that those individuals who are most dependent upon physical status—e.g.,

PROPORTION EMPLOYED, ACCORDING TO AGE, FOR FOUR
OCCUPATIONAL CLASSES, UNITED STATES, 1940

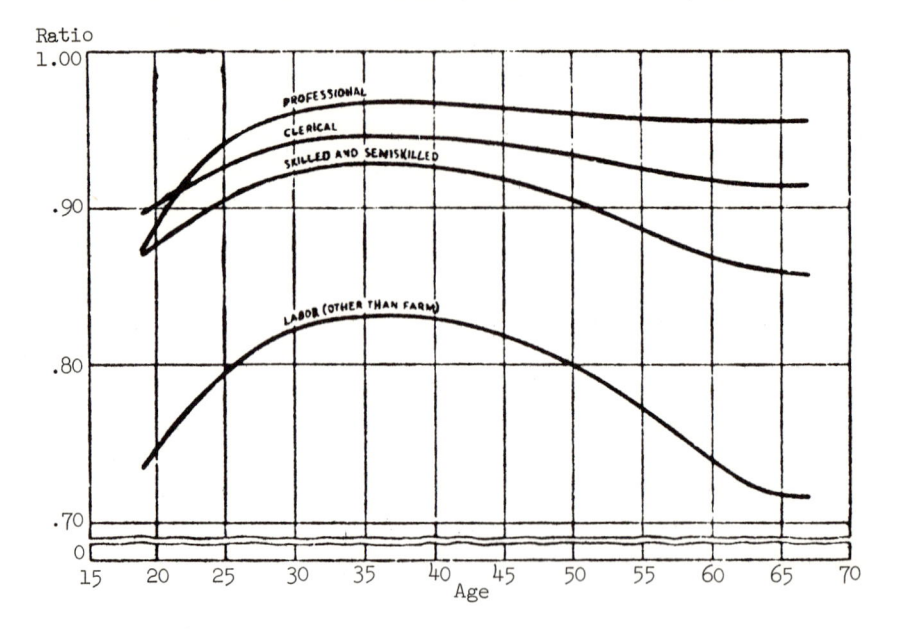

Figure 4. The differential threat of aging for various economic groups as reflected in age trends in the percentage employed in different categories at different ages. Data are for 1940, a time when cultural discrimination would likely be better reflected than in times of peak employment. (From L. I. Dublin and A. J. Lotka, The Money Value of a Man, revised ed., New York, Ronald Press, 1946.)

strength or attractiveness—have psychological curves closely approximating the biological curve of life, whereas those engaged in mental pursuits have a psychological curve lagging the physical curve. One would expect, for example, a narcissistic person, a chorus girl, or a prize fighter to feel the threat of age much earlier than a non-narcissistic person, a university professor, or a physician.

Differences in Degree of Future Orientation and Meaning of Life

A number of writers have commented on the fact that certain lives seem to have "unity," that certain individuals seem well integrated and "inner-directed." In contrast, other individuals seem responsive to the many situations in which they find themselves. Some people seem "future-oriented" and work toward deferred gratifications; others live essentially for the present. Such differences are likely to be especially, but not exclusively, evident in the different meanings that work and career have for different individuals.

Differences of this nature assume importance in evaluating the generality of "expansion" needs in human lives, and in assessing the overall character of motivational changes during the adult years. Filer and O'Connell (1962), for example, have noted that despite a mean gain among a group of oldsters under conditions of a useful contributing climate (a finding which, as noted earlier, was interpreted as failing to substantiate the "disengagement" hypothesis), some individuals made no gain and some lost. Quite properly these authors have noted that any theory of aging must encompass such contrasting trends among individuals. What seems "disengagement" may not really be this if the individual were not "engaged" psychologically to begin with. And, for others, "disengagement" may actually mean "re-engagement," in the sense of retiring "to" rather than "from." Investigations into the personal meanings with which different people invest their goals and their varied behaviors, and the relationship of the specifics of their lives, are much needed.

Of those psychologists interested in aging, Charlotte Buhler has probably been most interested in fathoming the meaning and unity of the course of human life, and of describing this meaning in terms of changing motivations, sequences of goals, and self-conceptions. In her most recent papers (1957, 1962), she has given special emphasis to the meaningfulness of life, self-realization, and fulfillment. For many people, she argues, life is a meaningful project involving self-determination toward goals, with various espisodes of self-assessment along the way, and ending in fulfillment or failure. Something of the range of individual differences is suggested by her categorization of those individuals interviewed (Buhler, 1961). Four groups were identified:

1. Those who felt they had done their lives' work and wanted to rest and relax and were content to do so.
2. Those who felt that their active life was never finished and who continued striving to the end.
3. Those who, though not satisfied with their lives and accomplishments, but lacking strength, ability or will-power to go on struggling, find an unhappy resignation.

4. Those who led thoughtless and meaningless lives, and who are now not only frustrated but bothered by guilt and regret.

In her overall evaluation, Buhler concluded that more critical in old age maladjustment than functional decline and insecurity is the individual's self-assessment as to whether he did or did not reach fulfillment. This she felt was true of the person who had hoped for accomplishments, but often, as well, for the person who did not think of his life as a whole at the outset but who later became aware of a pattern.

Although Buhler's generalizations reflect clinical impressions and are not so well-supported by empirical data as many psychologists might wish, her points seem well taken and square sufficiently with subjective observations and experiences to suggest an important area of research as well as hypotheses to give that research direction. The suggested focus is upon basic motivational tendencies, sequences of goals, meaningfulness and fulfillment—with attention to differences among individuals and the kinds of antecedent and concurrent conditions that have brought them about.

Basic Sources of Satisfaction and Adult Education

In his important book on personality published in 1938, Henry Murray introduced the concept of environmental "press," paralleling the concept of need for the individual. Not only was Murray concerned with the need patterns of individuals, he was interested in the potential of the environment for arousing and satisfying those needs. He suggested an important area of research related to analysis of the threat, and frustration, as well as potential satisfactions to be found in various environments. Generally speaking, it might be hypothesized that a person will seek out that type of environment which he perceives as having the potential of satisfying his needs. Thus, the need-press concept has important implications for understanding why people choose particular occupations, friends, or mates. (Or, for that matter, why they seek out and relate to any major aspect of their environment.)

Since a culture tends to be age-graded, and to offer different types of stimulation, satisfaction potential, and frustration to different age groups, it might well be anticipated that the concept of environmental press would also be especially useful in explaining age trends. Cycles of satisfaction and frustration in work or in marriage may be explained, for example, by changing need-press relationships. A job which satisfies at one period of life may not satisfy at a later time when one's psychological needs have changed, or one's capacities for achieving gratification of needs have altered.

These comments introduce the concluding section of this paper which relates to basic sources of satisfaction in life and their implication for adult education. It is almost self-evident that because of technological advances we not only have more leisure available but less opportunity for intrinsic satisfaction in one of the historically important areas of gratification: work. One important implication of this change is that other means of basic gratifications must be found. While this is an important challenge for American society, it also represents an opportunity for adult education institutions.

Applying the need-press concept to this situation, a major question concerns the degree to which adult education programs are perceived by adults as yielding opportunities for need-satisfaction. What little evidence we have is not encouraging. In one study, less than one per cent of the population reported going to lectures or adult schools "yesterday" (Kleemeier, 1961). And, as shown in recent census surveys, older people are proportionately less represented in adult education programs. These findings suggest that the general population, at least, does not have a positive image of such programs. A basic problem, then, would seem to involve the study of the character of the "image" people hold of adult education, particularly image as defined as the perceived need-satisfaction-potential of adult education.

Moving from the total perception of adult education to the curriculum, it is apparent that the motivations of adults, as they change with age, will have important implications for the program offered. Research directed to more detailed analysis of the goals of individuals, the avenues by which they satisfy expansion needs, as well as developmental tasks and sources of anxiety, will have important implications as to the nature of specific offerings appropriate for people in different phases of life.

Although a number of more recent studies support this general contention, the data collected by Smith (1924) reflect particularly well the different role adult education programs play in the lives of people of different ages. Courses were taken for vocational purposes more often in younger adult years but for "general cultural" purposes in later years. In somewhat different terminology, this implies that the courses taken in young adult years have instrumental value in the service of other motives or goals, whereas in later years when other avenues of expansion are blocked, people find intrinsic satisfaction in adult education. If motivational patterns of individuals are complex, equally complex is the potential of the sub-culture called adult education for the satisfaction of needs. Careful studies in depth of the relationships between person and program are much needed.

Finally, the findings on motivational changes with age have important meanings for adult education methodology. Particularly relevant is the increasing susceptibility to threat that characterizes older age groups, the resultant personality changes, and the implications these trends have for instructional procedures. The final paper in this book deals with such matters.

Summary

It has been suggested in this paper that hypothesizing two broad motivational patterns—one of growth and expansion, the other of anxiety and threat—will serve to integrate a wide variety of data reflecting developmental changes during the adult life span. The major points made in the development of this notion are as follows:

1. A number of factors interact to cause age changes in adult motivation. These include age-related differences in cultural stimulation and expectation, the degree to which satisfaction or chronic frustration of certain major motives over time paves the way for the emergence of other motives, and the degree to which people experience social and physical losses in highly valued areas. Becoming locked into a situation tends to make frustrations keener, and changing time perspectives create critical points in the motivational history of individuals.

2. The postulation of a need for growth-expansion integrates commonly observed goals and interests. One notes shifts in goals and interests from career and family, to community interests, to identification with children's success, to religious and philosophical interests. In general, although growth-expansion motives seem important throughout life, their satisfaction is by less direct and more vicarious means in older years. As age increases, there appears to be less personal investment

(ego-involvement, energy) in life and in the satisfaction of needs.

3. The recently advanced theory of disengagement, which suggests that people <u>seek</u> a disengaged state as something valued in its own right, seems not supported by the data, though this view is having a stimulating effect upon research.

4. The evidence seems particularly clear that anxiety and susceptibility to threat increase with the passage of time, and that this circumstance tends to be the motivational source for many of the behavioral (personality) changes that occur with age. This particular trend has important implications for adult education methodology.

5. Individual differences are, of course, important, and have been demonstrated with respect to sex and social-economic class. Among the important differences are the ages at which irreversible losses become evident, the degree to which one's life is seen as a meaningful pattern, and the ways in which various subgroups of the population translate their needs into specific goals or adapt particular patterns of defense against losses.

6. It was suggested, in conclusion, that technological advances which have created more leisure and fewer opportunities for satisfaction in work have resulted in important opportunities for adult education. In early years of adult life, education is used in the service of various expansion needs (e.g., career, family), but in later years adult education may well become a basic source of need satisfaction (an avenue of expansion). In any event, a careful analysis of the relation of adult education to the major motivational patterns of adult years, and to the types of developmental tasks pin-pointed by psychological research, would seem to have value.

References

Aging and the Aged, <u>The University of Chicago Reports</u>, Vol. 12, No. 2, Nov. 1961.

Atkin, S. Discussion of the paper by M. R. Kaufman, "Old age and aging: the psychoanalytic point of view." <u>Amer. J. Orthopsychiat.</u>, 1940, <u>10</u>, 79-83.

Barker, R. G. and L. S. The psychological ecology of old people in Midwest, Kansas, and Yoredale, Yorkshire. <u>J. Gerontol.</u>, 1961, <u>16</u>, 144-49.

Barron, M. The Aging American. New York: Crowell, 1961.

Bendig, A. W. Age differences in the interscale factor structure of the Guilford-Zimmerman Temperament Survey. J. consult. Psychol., 1960, 24, 134-38.

Britten, R. H. Sex differences in physical impairment in adult life. Amer. J. Hyg., 1931, 13, 741-70.

Brozek, J. Personality of young and middle-aged normal men: item analysis of a psychosomatic inventory. J. Gerontol., 1952, 7, 410-18.

Buhler, Charlotte. Genetic aspects of the self. Ann. N.Y. Acad. Sci., 1962, 96, 730-64.

Buhler, Charlotte. Der Menschliche Lebenslauf Als Psychologisches Problem. Leipzig: Verlag von S. Hirzel, 1933.

Buhler, Charlotte. Maturation and motivation. Personality, 1951, 1, 184-211.

Buhler, Charlotte. Meaningful leisure in the mature years, Chap. 12, pp. 345-87. In R. W. Kleemeier (ed.), Aging and Leisure, New York: Oxford University Press, 1961.

Buhler, Charlotte. Old age and fulfillment of life with considerations of the use of time in old age. Vita hum., Basel, 1961, 4, 129-33.

Buhler, Charlotte. Zur Psychologie des Menschlichen Lebenslaufes. Psychol. Rdsch., 1957, 8, 1-15.

Cavan, R. S., Burgess, E. W., Havighurst, R. J., and Goldhammer, H. Personal Adjustment in Old Age. Chicago: Science Research Associates, 1949.

Cumming, Elaine and Henry, W. E. Growing Old. New York: Basic Books, 1961.

Dean, Lois R. Aging and the decline of instrumentality. J. Gerontol., 1960, 15, 440-46.

Dykman, R. A., Heimann, E. K., and Kerr, W. A. Lifetime worry patterns of three diverse adult cultural groups. J. soc. Psychol., 1952, 35, 91-100.

Erikson, E. H. Identity and the Life Cycle. New York: International Universities Press, 1959.

Filer, R. N. and O'Connell, D. D. A useful contribution climate for the aging. J. Gerontol., 1962, 17, 51-57.

Gurin, G., Veroff, J., and Feld, Sheila. Americans View Their Mental Health: A Nationwide Interview Survey. New York: Basic Books, Inc., 1960.

Hamilton, G. V. Changes in personality and psychosexual phenomena with age. In E. V. Cowdry (ed.), Problems of Aging, Chap. XXX, 810-31. 2nd ed. Baltimore: Williams & Wilkins Co., 1942.

Havighurst, R. J. Who Shall Be Educated? New York: Longmans, Green, 1953.

Havighurst, R. J. and Albrecht, R. Older People. New York: Longmans, Green, 1953.

Johnson, G. H. Differences in the job satisfaction of urban teachers as related to age and other factors. (Unpublished Ph.D. dissertation, Syracuse University, 1951.)

Kaufman, M. R. Old age and aging: the psychoanalytic point of view. Amer. J. Orthopsychiat., 1940, 10, 73-79.

Kerr, W. A., Newman, H. L., and Sadewic, A. R. Lifetime worry patterns of American psychologists. J. consult. Psychol., 1949, 13, 377-80.

Kleemeier, R. W. Aging and Leisure. New York: Oxford University Press, 1961.

Kogan, N. and Wallach, M. A. Age changes in values and attitudes. J. Gerontol., 1961, 16, 272-80.

Kuhlen, R. G. Age trends in adjustment during the adult years as reflected in happiness ratings. Paper read at a meeting of the American Psychological Association, Boston, 1948.

Kuhlen, R. G. Expansion and constriction of activities during the adult years as reflected in organizational, civic and political participation. Paper read at Second International Gerontological Congress, St. Louis, 1951.

Kuhlen, R. G. Nervous symptoms among military personnel as related to age, combat experience and marital status. J. consult. Psychol., 1951, 15, 320-24.

Kuhlen, R. G. and Johnson, G. H. Changes in goals with increasing adult age. J. consult. Psychol., 1952, 16, 1-4.

Kutner, B., Fanshel, D., Togo, Alice M., and Langner, T. S. Five Hundred Over Sixty: A Community Survey on Aging. New York: Russell Sage Foundation, 1956.

Landis, J. T. What is the happiest period of life? Sch. Soc., 1942, 55, 643-45.

Lehman, H. C. Age and Achievement. Princeton, N.J.: Princeton Univ. Press, 1953.

Lehner, G. F. J. and Gunderson, E. K. Height relationships on the Draw-a-Person Test. J. Pers., 1953, 21, 392-99.

Lewin, K. Field theory and experiment in social psychology. Amer. J. of Sociol., 1939, 44, 868-96.

Maslow, A. H. A theory of human motivation. Psychol. Rev., 1943, 50, 370-96.

Mason, Evelyn P. Some correlates of self-judgments of the aged. J. Gerontol., 1954, 9, 324-37.

McClelland, D. C. The Achievement Motive. New York: Appleton-Century-Crofts, 1953.

Morgan, Christine M. The attitudes and adjustments of recipients of old age assistance in upstate and metropolitan New York. Arch. Psychol., 1937, No. 214.

Murray, H. A. Explorations in Personality. New York: Oxford University Press, 1938.

Neugarten, B. L. and Gutmann, D. L. Age-sex roles and personality in middle age: a thematic apperception study. Psychol. Monogr., 1958, 72 (17, Whole No. 470).

Norman, R. D. Concealment of age among psychologists: evidence for a popular stereotype. J. Psychol., 1949, 30, 127-35.

Olsen, I. A. and Elder, J. H. A word-association test of emotional disturbance in older women. J. Gerontol., 1958, 13, 305-8.

Phillips, B. S. A role theory approach to adjustment in old age. Amer. sociol. Rev., 1957, 22, 212-17.

Powell, M. and Ferraro, C. D. Sources of tension in married and single women teachers of different ages. J. educ. Psychol., 1960, 51, 92-101.

Reissman, L. Levels of aspiration and social class. Amer. sociol. Rev., 1953, 18, 233-42.

Rosen, J. L. and Neugarten, B. L. Ego functions in the middle and later years: thematic apperception study of normal adults. J. Gerontol., 1960, 15, 62-67.

Schaie, K. W. The effect of age on a scale of social responsibility. J. soc. Psychol., 1959, 5, 221-24.

Scott, J. P., Fredericson, E., and Fuller, J. L. Experimental exploration of the critical period hypothesis. Personality, 1951, 1, 162-83.

Simmons, L. W. Attitudes toward aging and the aged: primitive societies. J. Gerontol., 1946, 1, 72-95.

Strong, E. K., Jr. Vocational Interests of Men and Women. Stanford, Calif.: Stanford University Press, 1943.

Sward, K. Age and mental ability in superior men. Amer. J. Psychol., 1945, 58, 443-70.

Tobin, S. S. and Neugarten, B. L. Life satisfaction and social interaction in the aging. J. Gerontol., 1961, 16, 344-46.

Tobin, S. S. and Neugarten, Bernice L. Life satisfaction and social interaction in the aging. J. Gerontol., 1961, 16, 344-46.

Tuckman, J. and Lorge, I. The best years in life: a study in ranking. J. Psychol., 1952, 34, 137-49.

Veroff, J., Atkinson, J. W., Feld, S. C., and Curin, G. The use of thematic apperception to assess motivation in a nationwide interview study. Psychol. Monogr., 1960, 74 (12, Whole No. 499).

Veroff, J., Feld, Sheila, and Gurin, G. Dimensions of subjective adjustment. J. abnorm. and soc. Psychol., 1962, 64, 192-205.

Wallach, M. A. and Kogan, N. Aspects of judgment and decision making: Inter-relationships and changes with age. Behav. Sci., 1961, 6, 23-36.

Welford, A. G. Skill and Age. London: Oxford University Press, 1951.

V

PSYCHOLOGICAL CHARACTERISTICS OF ADULTS AND INSTRUCTIONAL METHODS IN ADULT EDUCATION[1]

W. J. McKeachie
University of Michigan

The "results" sections of studies on teaching effectiveness seldom deviate from the familiar refrain: "no significant difference." Although the overall picture of research on teaching effectiveness is not so dismal as usually believed, we have not yet discovered a teaching method which is universally effective in achieving all educational goals for all types of students. It seems likely that what is effective for one student may be ineffective for others. Thus if we are to improve teaching we need to develop clearer understanding of how different kinds of students learn.

The Learning Situation

Students enter an adult education course with a number of important, relatively stable motives learned at home, in previous educational experiences, and through experiences with peers. There are not only individual differences in these motives but also differences in the relative strength of motives within individuals. Students also possess skills useful in achieving their educational goals. Some of these, such as verbal ability, are measured by intelligence tests; others like reading ability, note-taking, study habits, and ability to gain the instructor's sympathy or to make friends, are not so commonly measured. The student's learning depends both upon his motives and his skills for satisfaction of his motives.

I know very little about the communication channels through which

---

[1] The author acknowledges with gratitude the stimulation and criticism of other members of the staff of the U.S. Office of Education Cooperative Research Project O.E. #SAE-8541, particularly co-directors, J. E. Milholland and R. L. Isaacson.

adults learn about educational opportunities or what attracts them to adult education. I am sure, however, that those in adult education programs are not a random sample but are selected from the population because of motives which they believe can be satisfied by the course for which they have enrolled. This means that each adult class is made up of individuals having certain special needs and with expectations about the functions adult education will serve.

Environmental Press

The total environment of the student has much to do with activating motives and skills. Pace and Stern (1958) have shown that colleges differ markedly in their students' perceptions of what are important goals and appropriate instrumental behaviors to attain these goals. Presumably there are comparable differences in the environment characterizing different settings of adult education. Some settings of adult education, for example, may emphasize practical vocational values; others may reinforce social, affiliative values; others may stress intellectual concerns. But in contrast to residential colleges, the adult education program has little control over the total environment. The attitudes of family, friends, and co-workers are likely to be potent in determining what motives are dominant, and in determining what demands are competing for the student's study and class time.

In addition to general expectations about adult education the student develops specific expectations about the likely satisfactions and appropriate instrumental behaviors in his classes. The cues provided by his instructors may activate motives or skills which have previously been latent, may maintain the activation of motives or skills already active, may frustrate expectations previously elicited by the total environment, or may arouse uncertainty and anxiety about the likelihood of success or failure in reaching his goals.

Strategy

Because of the conflicting demands upon his time, the student must develop a strategy[2] such as maximizing satisfaction or minimizing regret. Since the student is involved in several activities in which voca-

---

2. The word "strategy" implies a greater degree of consciousness and rationality than I intend. Clearly much of the process is unconscious and intuitive.

tional, family, and recreational demands are competing with the demands of his class, his strategy must involve assessment of the potential rewards and punishments and the probabilities of attainment of his goals in each of these situations. Whatever his strategy, its choice involves an assessment of his habits and skills in relation both to the possible satisfactions in the situation and to the types of behavior necessary to achieve these satisfactions. From this assessment comes an estimate both of the amount and kind of satisfaction, and the probability of attaining it in class. Both of these factors are important in determining his active motivation to learn.

Skills

The individual's habits and skills thus enter into motivation in determining subjective probability. But they also enter into predictions of achievement again in their own right, for the achievement of a student depends not only upon his <u>estimate</u> of the likelihood that he will achieve his goals but also upon his <u>actual</u> skill.

The individual's habits and skills also enter into our theory of academic learning in a third term. In discussing the academic environment, we noted that the total environment develops motivational and instrumental expectancies which the student brings into the classroom. When these expectancies are not fulfilled, frustration may result. For example announcement of an especially rigorous grading policy is almost invariably greeted with groans of dismay and an upsurge in frustration-instigated behavior. But the instructor who blocks or de-emphasizes such usual instrumental responses as note taking, memorizing a given textbook, or answering specific factual test items is likely to encounter even stronger resistance. We would expect the blocking of old learning habits and the demand for developing new ones to be especially frustrating and anxiety producing for the older student. It may simply be that the instructor who emphasizes different instrumental responses produces frustration because he is lowering the student's subjective probability of success; it may be that frustration results because one's well learned habits come to have secondary motivational values in themselves; or it may be that any marked change of expectancy is unpleasant. In any case, lack of confirmation of habit-skill expectancies may be frustrating, and frustration in turn may have certain responses associated with it which interfere with learning.

Learning Factors

How much the student's activities contribute to his learning will presumably also depend upon the teacher's skill in programming to achieve course objectives for each student. An effective learning program for some students may not be equally effective learning for others.

Some learning theorists and educators would agree that present day learning theory has little relevance for education. Learning theory, based on tightly controlled experiments in which the learning is measured by speed of running, rate of bar pressing, or turning left or right, is ill-equipped to deal with the complexities of the classroom learning of mature adults. Nevertheless, basic principles have emerged which seem to apply fairly generally to learning, and which can provide a helpful background for understanding the relation between educational effectiveness and personal characteristics. By isolating and observing the effects of variables in the laboratory situation, we are better able to predict their operation in natural situations where the many variables interacting tend to cloud the effect of any one variable. Some variables which are now generally seen to be important are discussed in the following sections.

Motivation

Student learning and memory are closely tied to motivation. Students are more likely to learn what they want to learn than material in which they are not interested. To be useful this principle of motivation needs to be accompanied with information about dependable motives of adult students. We know that motives vary with age, sex, social class, and other social variables. Motivation for satisfying family relationships is likely to be high among adults (Havighurst and Orr, 1956). Most students want to be liked. Zander's interview study of adult students (1951) revealed affiliation to be one of the strongest conscious motives for taking an evening course. A third important motive of adult learners is need for achievement. Among adults who seek additional educational experiences are likely to be many motivated by the sheer joy of accomplishment. For these, we would expect the challenge of an unsolved problem or of a task with chance of success to be highly motivating (Atkinson, 1958). Others see education as instrumental to other achievement goals.

Many students have conflicting motives. Even among adults one common conflict is between independence and dependence. Students are likely to resent the teacher who directs their activities too closely but they are also likely to be anxious when given independence. The teacher then has the problem of simultaneously satisfying both motives. As a result of this conflict some students disagree with the teacher not on rational grounds but simply as a way of expressing emotions. Similarly, student apathy may be an irrational expression of resentment about being required to do anything.

Any thoughtful teacher of adults could list many more student motives. The point here is simply that these motives provide the tools by which teachers get learning to take place, and that individual differences in these motives affect learning.

It probably does not matter what motives are aroused, but this does not mean that the type of motivation used is unimportant for speed of learning. Evidence has accumulated to suggest that negative and positive motives may affect behavior. Teachers often use mixtures of positive and negative motives. When negative motives predominate, students will work hard if that is the only way to avoid undesirable consequences. But, if there are other ways out of the situation, students will take them. In adult classes heavy use of threat is likely to lead students to drop the course.

The closer the goal or threatened danger, the higher the motivation. Negative motives are sometimes not as affective outside the learning situation as are positive motives because the effectiveness of fear is often more dependent upon the closeness of the goal than is the effectiveness of positive motives. Moreover negative motives lead to avoidance of or withdrawal from the anxiety arousing situation. A study by Atkinson and Litwin (1960) showed that male students who were high in anxiety about tests as measured by the Mandler-Sarason test anxiety questionnaire and the Thematic Apperception Test, were among the first to complete the course examination and did poorer work on the examination than in their work during the course. Students with positive motivation to succeed tended to stay in the examination room longer.

To sum up the argument thus far: motivation is important in learning. We can use student motivation for success or approval to produce learning. Threats of punishment or of withdrawal of satisfaction are likely to produce withdrawal or other maladaptive responses.

Organization

A teacher's job is not done when he interests his class, for the amount students learn depends at least in part upon the amount he teaches. But this relationship is not so simple as it may at first appear. It may well be that the more we teach the less our students learn!

In the Great Didactic, Comenius writes, "If we take a jar with a narrow mouth (for to this we may compare a boy's intellect) and attempt to pour a quantity of water into it violently, instead of allowing it to trickle in drop by drop, what will be the results? Without a doubt the greater part of the liquid will flow over the side, and ultimately the jar will contain less than if the operation had taken part gradually. Quite as foolish is the action of those who try to teach their pupils not as much as they can assimilate, but as much as they themselves wish."

Comenius would not have been surprised by the work of David Katz (1950), the German-Swedish psychologist who devised a number of unique experiments demonstrating that beyond a certain point adding to the elements in an intellectual task causes confusion and inefficiency.

Fortunately, it is possible to teach more and have it remembered better. The magic formula is "organization." As Katona (1940) demonstrated in a series of experiments on organization and memory, we can learn and remember much more when our learning fits into an organization or fills a gap. The successful teacher is one whose students can thoroughly visualize meaningful problems. The ideal class begins with a problem so important that the students are always just a step ahead of the teacher in approaching a solution.

Thus motivation and organization are two key concepts which can guide efforts to help students acquire knowledge.

Variability and Verbalization

How can we aid in developing principles and concepts for students to apply broadly? Many teachers have been disheartened by seeing a student answer a routine problem perfectly and then fail to use the same knowledge in solving a new problem where it is relevant. There have been a number of educational attempts to solve this problem. One early slogan was, "Learning by doing." The theory of learning by doing was that if one learned something in the situation where the learning was to be used one would not have the added step of learning when to apply it.

At first glance, this seems perfectly reasonable, and even makes sense psychologically. But the number of situations in which one must use knowledge is infinite, and one cannot learn by doing in all of them. Our goal must be to develop generalizations.

We develop generalizations from specific instances in <u>varying</u> contexts. A number of experiments have demonstrated that repetitive drill is much less effective than varying problems in developing principles which can be applied to new situations (e.g., Wolfle, 1935). <u>Verbalization</u> can help us identify the common elements in these situations and shorten the learning process. While teacher verbalization of principles is undoubtedly better than unresolved confusion, Kersh (1958) suggests, on the basis of his research, that allowing students themselves to discover principles may enhance motivation, and Lahti (1956) found inductive methods to be particularly effective for students with a poor background.

<u>Feedback and Active Learning</u>

If students are to learn skills, they have to practice, but practice alone does not make perfect. Practice works only if the learner <u>sees the results</u> of his practice, i.e., if he receives feedback.

A number of experiments demonstrate that <u>active</u> learning is more efficient than passive learning. (McGeoch and Irion, 1952). One reason for this may be the improved opportunities for feedback in active learning. Discussion techniques may help develop critical thinking because students do the thinking and there is an opportunity to check their thinking against that of others. But one danger of "student-centered" or "nondirective" discussion is that the <u>results</u> are not apparent. Students may make comments, express opinions, and participate actively, but their opinions may be no more informed at the end of a semester than at the beginning.

Nevertheless we need to go a step beyond the principle that students learn what they practice with knowledge of results. It is not always easy to get students to practice critical thinking in the classroom. The student who remains quiet in class avoids the risk of disagreement, criticism, and embarrassment. To develop motivation, teachers need to pose problems within the range of their students' abilities. Studies of the development of achievement motivation in children indicate that parents develop this motivation by encouraging the child to do well and setting standards which the child can achieve. Other parents who orient their children toward achievement fail because they set unreasonable goals.

One misconception of adult educators who have recognized the importance of motivation, is that they sometimes stop with the motives students already have. Adults are neither too old to learn new motives nor to strengthen old ones.

Learning: A Summary

Learning depends upon values and norms of the total culture of which the adult course is a part, upon the students' motives and skills, upon cues from the teacher's activating motives and skills, and upon the teacher's using such principles of learning as organization and feedback.

The Criterion Problem

Our discussion of motives and learning factors has already implied a major consideration in evaluating the effectiveness of differing teaching methods with different kinds of students. Students have different goals and a variety of teaching procedures are effective for particular kinds of learning. This means that one can seldom say that a particular teaching method is best, without qualification. Rather we can hope to say that Method A is effective for a particular kind of student in achieving Objective I, but not as effective for other groups of students, or for achieving Objective II.

The criterion problem is illustrated by the experiment of Parsons, Ketcham, and Beach (1958). Groups of students who did not come to class did better than those who attended class on the final examination. The catch is that the examination was based entirely upon the textbook. As the authors point out, their results with the other groups suggest that the more new ideas and points of view are introduced, the less likely students are to remember what the textbook says. If our goal is for the student to remember the textbook, a test on the textbook is appropriate, but we cannot conclude that a particular method is superior in achieving all goals, if we have measured only one. This criterion problem is particularly acute in adult courses where, as we have already seen, there may be a wide variety of student and instructor goals.

The difficulty in arriving at an over-all index of teaching effectiveness is complicated by the probability that a teacher effective in achieving one course objective is not necessarily effective in achieving others. Bendig (1955), for example, found a significant interaction between instructors and tests in an introductory psychology course. Some instructors' students did well on certain tests during the course but not well on other tests. Cross (1958) and McKeachie (1959) found that students who did well on an objective test in psychology were ineffective when their achievement was measured on an essay test designed to measure understanding and integration of the materials. In considering alternative teaching methods it is thus important to specify objectives.

Because achievement measures have been insensitive to differences in teaching methods, most research stresses favorable student reactions to new methods. Although the relationship between student satisfaction and learning is low (Elliott, 1950), it can certainly be argued that assuming equal learning between two methods, we would prefer to have students leave our classes with warm feelings about their experiences. Moreover we would expect this feeling to be related to interest in learning more; there is some evidence to support this expectation (McKeachie and Solomon, 1958). When, however, we use student satisfaction as a criterion, we should be aware of the fact that it is highly influenced by students' role expectations. Laboratory studies of problem solving groups reveal that authoritarian leaders are rated by group members as being more efficient than democratic leaders (Haythorn, et al., 1956). A leader who plays an active role is almost inevitably going to be more salient in his impression on a group than a leader whose behavior is more suble. In evaluating student reactions, one therefore needs to be conscious of these role expectancies and to determine a proper base line against which to evaluate the reactions.

With these caveats in mind, let us look at some common teaching methods and their likely effectiveness for differing types of students.

Teaching Methods and Personal Characteristics

In considering personal characteristics of students as they affect effective teaching, one might organize his materials either in terms of teaching methods or of student characteristics. In this paper both approaches will be used, first reviewing different teaching methods in terms of student characteristics which might condition their effectiveness, then turning to student characteristics which affect learning.

Lecturing

College teaching and lecturing have so long been associated that when one pictures a college professor in a classroom, he almost inevitably pictures him as lecturing. Since lectures typically provide few opportunities for students to respond, there is little opportunity for students to receive feedback except through periodic tests. Delay of feedback may not be a major factor in learning if the student is motivated and the material is not too difficult. We would, however, expect lack of feedback to be a greater handicap if the lecturer's goal is to develop concepts or problem solving skills. With these goals there is experimental evidence that active participation on the part of the learner is more effective than passive listening or observing.

What type of student would we expect to benefit most from lectures? In terms of the theory presented earlier we might expect them to be students low in need for dominance, power, and affiliation. Those with strong dominance, power, or affiliation motives find few opportunities to satisfy them during a lecture. Unfortunately, conclusive data supporting or refuting these hypotheses is lacking. The one study finding a personality characteristic related to success in lecture is that of Beach (1960), who studied the personality variable of sociability as a predictor of achievement in lecture and small-group teaching methods. In the lecture section the non-sociable students (as measured by the Guilford Inventory of Factors STDCR) achieved significantly more than the sociable students; in the small-group sections the results were reversed.

Discussion Methods

Discussion technique may be ill-suited for communicating information because the rate of communication of information from instructor to student is slow. When information encounters intellectual or emotional resistance, however, discussion methods may bring the source of resistance to light. Adults are likely to have built up more emotional associations than younger students. Thus dealing with emotional resistance may be more important in adult classes than in those with younger students.

Moreover if students are to achieve application, critical thinking, or some of the other higher cognitive objectives, it seems reasonable to assume that they should have an opportunity to practice these skills. While teaching machines are designed to provide prompt and realistic feedback, a group discussion permits presentation of a variety of problems enabling a number of people to gain experience in integrating facts, formulating hypotheses, amassing relevant evidence, and evaluating conclusions. In fact the prompt feedback provided by the teaching machine may actually be less effective than a method in which students are encouraged to discover solutions for themselves with less step-by-step guidance (Della Piana, 1956). Since problem solving ordinarily requires information, we might expect discussion to be more effective for groups with more information than those lacking in background. Since one of the assets of the adult class is the wide variety of experiences of its members, discussion techniques may be particularly helpful in using these resources.

In extreme forms of student-centered or non-directive teaching, the teacher never evaluates contributions, never gives direction, and tries to become a neutral group leader. Such a method might be expected to have serious weaknesses, at least in achieving lower-level cognitive-level goals, such as knowledge of facts. With the instructor's role as information giver reduced, his role as source of feedback virtually eliminated, and his opportunity to provide organization and structure curtailed, it is apparent that a heavy burden falls upon the group members to carry out these functions. We would expect that they could best be assumed by groups which not only have some background in the academic discipline involved but also have had experience in carrying out these functions in "democratic" groups. We would guess that authoritarian students would be unhappy and anxious in such classes. Similarly classes with a high proportion of individuals reluctant to participate will be fun for neither student nor teacher. Zander (1951) found lack of student participation to be a common complaint of teachers of adult classes.

A number of experiments testing student-centered teaching have been carried out with essentially negative results (Landsman, 1950; Jenkins, 1952; Bills, 1952; Johnson and Smith, 1953; Slomowitz, 1955; Deignan, 1955; Rasmussen, 1956; Krumboltz and Farquar, 1957). The Johnson and Smith study is one of the few to provide support for our suggestion that the success of student-centered teaching depends upon previous group experiences of the students. They suggested that the critical factor in the success of one democratic class was the enthusiastic participation of a member of a student cooperative. Since many adult learners have had experience in discussion or problem solving groups, one might have a better chance of success with discussion in adult than in other classes.

Patton (1955) felt that an important variable in student-centered classes was the students' acceptance of responsibility for learning. In his experiment, he compared traditional classes with two classes in which there were no examinations, no lectures, and no assigned readings. Students in the experimental classes decided what readings they would do, what class procedures would be used, what they would hand in, and how they would be graded. At the end of the course, the students in these classes, as compared to the control group, (1) felt that the course was more valuable, (2) showed greater interest in psychology, and (3) tended to give more dynamic, motivational analyses of a behavior problem. But giving students power cannot work if they will not accept responsibility; so Patton also obtained individual measures of acceptance of responsibility within the experimental classes. As hypothesized, he found that the degree to which the student accepted responsibility was positively correlated with gain in psychological knowledge, gain in ability to apply psychology, rating of the value of the course, and interest in psychology.

What sort of student will accept responsibility in such a course? Patton found that the students who liked his experimental class and assumed responsibility were likely to be independent of traditional authority figures and high in need for achievement. Koenig and McKeachie (1959) similarly found that women high in need for achievement preferred independent study to lectures.

A pioneering step in the direction of relating personality to response to discussion methods was taken by Wispe (1951) who used TAT-like measures to differentiate three types of students: the personality-insecure student (51 per cent of the sample); the satisfied student (26 per cent of the sample); and the independent student (23 per cent of the sample). The insecure student had unfavorable attitudes toward instructors, fellow students, and both directive and permissive teaching, no matter what method his instructor used. The independent student had moderately favorable attitudes toward students and instructors, but was likely to direct aggression against the instructor in directive classes.

In their study of Springfield College students, Ashmus and Haigh (1952) found, as contrasted with Wispe, almost equal numbers choosing non-directive and directive methods. Students choosing non-directive classes did not differ from students choosing directive classes in intelligence or grades, but were more likely to have had previous experience in non-directive groups and tended to be more flexible, to be better able to cope with ambiguity, and to have more self-insight (Haigh and Schmidt, 1956).

Grading

One of the major problems in introducing non-directive or other new discussion methods is grading. Among adult classes, the problem of competition for grades is sometimes less acute than in college classes. Schwertman suggests (in Miller, 1960) that adults both fear course grades and want to be evaluated. Thus grading practices may have an important bearing upon the success of any teaching method, particularly a new one.

Complicating the problem of grading is the probability that low grades produce different effects upon different students. Waterhouse and Child (1953) did find that frustration produced deterioration in performance for subjects showing high interference tendencies, but produced improved performance for those with low interference tendencies. Interference tendencies were assessed by a questionnaire in which the subjects were asked to check on a 6-point scale the degree to which 90 responses to frustration were characteristic of himself.

Considering the importance of grading to both students and instructors, it is regrettable that there is so little empirical research. What kinds of students are affected most by grading policies? How do students learn to evaluate themselves? How do they learn to set goals for themselves? Do differing grading procedures facilitate or block such learning? To these questions we have no answers.

Homogeneous vs. Heterogeneous Grouping

One common criticism of discussion classes is that class time is wasted either by discussion of problems raised by the able students which are beyond the ken of the other students or by problems raised by the poor students which the other students feel are too elementary.

Because adult classes are frequently heterogeneous, research on homogeneous vs. heterogeneous groupings is of particular relevance to our problem of finding the most effective teaching methods. One of the early college experiments on ability grouping showed no significant advantages for homogeneous grouping by intelligence and even a trend toward the opposite results (Longstaff, 1932). The two earliest researches (Burtt et al., 1923, and Ullrich, 1926) reported results which seem reasonable. They both concluded that homogeneous groups were not superior to heterogeneous groups when given standard material but did superior work when the bright students were pushed. Similarly Tharp (1930) found homogeneous grouping to be superior in an analytic geometry course. All in all, it seems safe to conclude that homogeneous grouping by ability is profitable, if teaching makes use of the known characteristics of the group.

Homogeneous grouping by personality proved to be ineffective in the experiment in group problem solving reported by Hoffman (1959). Comparing groups of four students who were similar in personality profiles on the Guilford-Zimmerman to groups of dissimilar students, he found that the heterogeneous groups produced superior solutions. Hoffman suggests that heterogeneous groups are more likely to propose a variety of alternatives permitting inventive solutions.

In a study by Stern and Cope (Stern, 1962) groups of "authoritarian, anti-authoritarian, and rational" students in a citizenship course were segregated into homogeneous groups in which the instructor was unaware of which kind of group he was teaching. Authoritarian students in the experimental group achieved more than comparable authoritarians in conventional classes.

It is apparent that we need further analysis of what kinds of homogenieties or heterogeneties contribute to certain objectives. It may be that the potential advantages of carefully planned grouping have not been realized simply because we have not yet learned optimal teaching procedures for such groups. From a theoretical point of view the importance of group size and heterogeneity in a discussion class depends upon the purpose of the discussion. If, for example, one is interested in using group members as sources of information or of differing points of view, the larger and more heterogeneous the group, the greater its resources. On the other hand, the degree to which a group uses its resources depends upon communication. It is not only apparent that a smaller proportion of group members can participate in a larger group but also that members are less likely to volunteer their contribution in large heterogeneous groups. A final problem is that of group pressures toward consensus and conformity. One of the barriers to effective group problem solving is the tendency of a group to accept the majority view with insufficient consideration of minority views. Homogeneous groups may this be ineffective because they agree too easily.

Project Methods and Independent Study

The recent interest in independent study as a means of using faculty time more efficiently has brought forth a teaching method used in some form for many years. If one goal of education is to develop the ability to continue learning, it seems reasonable that the student should have supervised experience in learning independently—experience in which the instructor helps the student learn how to formulate problems, find answers, and evaluate his progress himself. One might expect the values of independent study to be greatest for students with high ability and with a good deal of background in the area to be covered since such students should be less likely to be overwhelmed by difficulties encountered.

Independent study programs frequently involve projects in which a student undertakes to gather and integrate data relative to some more-or-less important problem. The results of research on the effectiveness of the project method are not particularly encouraging. One of the first "independent study" experiments was that of Seashore (1928). Final examination scores, however, were no different for students carrying out individual projects than for students taught by the usual lecture-discussion method (Scheidemann, 1929). In a college botany course, Novak found (1958) that students in conventional classes learned more facts than did those taught by the project method. The project method was particularly ineffective for students in the middle third of the group intelligence. Similarly Goldstein (1956) reports that students taught in a standard laboratory did not learn more than students who were taught pharmacology by the project method. In a mental hygiene class, Timmel (1955) found no difference in the effectiveness of the lecture and project methods in changing adjustment. One morsel of support for the method comes from Thistlewaite's (1960) finding that National Merit Scholars checked requirement of a term paper or laboratory project as one characteristic of their most stimulating course.

In a well-controlled experiment at Oberlin (McCollough and Van Atta, 1958) students in introductory science, psychology, and mathematics were required to work independently of the instructor in small groups. As in an Antioch experiment (Churchill and Baskin, 1958) no significant differences in learning appeared, either as measured by the usual achievement tests or by tests of learning resourcefulness. Generally Oberlin students seem not to have been unhappy about the independent study although they indicated that they would have preferred several two-week periods of independent study to the single longer period. Although a number of personality characteristics did not affect performance, students who were less rigid and low in need of social support tended to profit relatively more from independent study than other students. Gruber and Weitman (1962) similarly found that students who did well in independent study valued academic independence, a result similar to that of Patton discussed earlier, and also supported by a study of a small sample of Carleton students enrolled in independent study (McKeachie, unpublished).

In studies of a child development course (Parsons, 1957, and Parsons, Ketcham, and Beach, 1958) four teaching methods were compared —lecture, instructor-led discussion, autonomous groups which did not come to class, and individual independent study in which each student was sent home with the syllabus, returning for the final examination. Students in the independent study group scored highest on an examination of factual material in the textbook. The authors explain their results in terms of the independent group's freedom from distraction of interesting examples, possible applications, or points of view opposing those presented in the text.

This study was unique in comparing the effect of independent study on both college and adult classes. The adult class came out quite differently. The adults were teachers commuting to campus for a Saturday class. In this case the adult students in independent study performed significantly worse than other groups on the examination. Perhaps these adults were less committed to regular study and had poorer conditions for carrying out independent study; they may also have experienced more frustration in not having a class after having made a commitment to come for it. For adults, study may be more a part time extra activity than for students on campus.

Automated Techniques

The impending shortage of college teachers has sparked several hotly contested skirmishes about the virtues or vices of various techniques of teaching with devices substituting for a portion of the usual face-to-face interaction between instructors and students.

Television reduces the opportunity for students to communicate with teachers. We would thus expect the effectiveness of television to vary inversely with the importance of two-way communication for feedback to the student, for social reinforcers, and for feedback to the teacher. What sort of students need such interpersonal feedback? We would guess that students with little skill in the subject matter area, students with high need for affiliation, and students with needs for recognition and power would be detrimentally affected by the use of television in place of a live teacher. Unfortunately no data is available to test these hypotheses.

A major project in closed-circuit instruction was that at Miami University (Macomber and Siegel, 1956, 1957, 1960). This group's research is of particular interest because it compared closed circuit television both with large lecture classes and small semi-discussion classes, and because the Miami staff studied the possible differential effect of different types of instruction upon students of differing abilities and attitudes. Student ability generally did not make a difference in the relative effectiveness of television. At Miami low-ability students in "Foundations of Human Behavior" and "Government" achieved more in conventional classes than in television classes, but in physiology and zoology, the opposite was true. However, student ratings of television instruction were inversely correlated with student ability. While the best television instructors were liked by all types of students, the better students ordinarily disliked television and large classes more than did the poorer students. Seibert (1958), however, found poorer performance in the television classes than in live classes for low ability students.

The latest innovation to hit the educational world is programed learning. Programed materials may be presented either in workbook format or in teaching machines. The term, teaching machine, refers to a device for presenting content and questions in predetermined sequences and providing immediate knowledge of results to an active learner. The successive questions proceed in tiny steps from the simple to the complex. The program of the lesson may include hints or other guidance.

Teaching machines or programed workbooks thus have several theoretical advantages over lecturing or other conventional methods of instruction and would seem to be particularly useful in expanding the scope of education for adults. Adult students might be brought to a common level of mastery of the fundamentals of a course through programed instruction enabling class periods to be used more profitably than in drill.

Unfortunately, there has been relatively little experimental work at the college and adult level to determine the usefulness of programed materials. Of particular interest to us are studies of individual difference variables affecting learning from programed materials. Skinner and his followers have generally minimized the role of individual differences, suggesting that with a properly constructed program, the same achievement level will be attained by all students, the only differences being in the amount of time taken to complete the program.

Little attention has been given to motivational factors influencing the effectiveness of programed learning. The assumption is made that prompt confirmation of correct responses will be motivating. However, Atkinson suggests that maximum achievement motivation occurs when success or failure is uncertain. If this is correct, the high percentage of correct answers for which programs are currently designed should be unmotivating, and we would expect those with strong achievement motives to be bored. On the other hand the high proportion of successes might be helpful in building a stronger hope of success in individuals dominated by fear of failure.[3]

Teaching Methods and Personal Characteristics: A Summary

It is clear that research on interactions between teaching methods and student characteristics has far to go. What evidence is available suggests that sociable students perform better in discussion groups than lecture classes. Independent, non-rigid students like and do well in teach-

---
3. Teevan and others at Bucknell are currently testing these hypotheses.

ing methods in which they are given responsibility, such as discussion and independent study.

Characteristics of Adult Learners

Before considering specific psychological characteristics it is encouraging to note that when an instructor is aware of the nature of differences among his students, his teaching is more effective. In an experiment in which teachers of physics were given increased knowledge of their students' personal background for one of their two classes, the students made significantly greater gains in achievement and rated their instructors as being more effective (Sturgis, 1958).

Intelligence

Intelligence is the one characteristic which consistently predicts educational achievement. But here our interest is not whether or not intelligent students do better than less intelligent students, but rather which teaching methods are particularly effective for the ablest students, and which for the less able. Guetzkow, Kelly, and McKeachie (1954) found that students differing in intelligence or in preferences for teaching methods were not differently affected by the three methods used in their study. Hudelson (1928) found similar results in his studies of class size. Macomber and Siegel's results (1956, 1957-a,b, 1960) reveal a tendency for high ability students to gain more in course-related attitudes in small rather than large sections. Other personality measures do not, however, predict differential achievement in large and small classes.

Ward's (1956) results also suggest that the ablest students benefit most from small groups. Comparing group study and lecture-demonstration methods in physical science courses, he found that the group methods resulted in better achievement on a measure of understanding and problem solving for the abler students. Less able students, however, benefited more from lecture-demonstration. Gruber and Weitman (1962) found that students below the median in intelligence did much better on a test requiring complex thought and independent learning if they had been assigned to an independent study section rather than given conventional instruction in a course in physical optics. Parsons, Ketcham, and Beach (1960) report that abler students are less satisfied the less they have responsibility for setting goals of learning. Wispe (1951) found that the poorer students made greater gains in directive classes than in student-centered classes. Calvin, Hoffman, and Harden (1957) also found in three experiments that less intelligent students consistently did better in group problem-solving situations conducted in an authoritarian manner than in groups conducted in a permissive manner. The same difference did not occur for bright students. Remmers (1933) found that poorer students did better with two lectures and one recitation than with three recitations per week.

McKeachie (1961) found that men with low intelligence do poorer in classes in which there is a good deal of student assertion of point of view than in those with less opportunity for assertiveness. Men with high intelligence do relatively better in the classes with high student assertiveness. Thus it appears that face-to-face discussion teaching is more advantageous for the more intelligent students than for those with less ability.

Anxiety and Sex Differences

One of the most active intersections of experimental psychology and experimental study of personality has been the area involving the effect of anxiety upon learning. The impetus for much of this work came from deductions from Hullian theory by Spence and Taylor (1951). Essentially this theory suggests that a high level of anxiety will facilitate simple learning, but beyond an optimal point will hamper complex learning (Sarason, 1960). Since academic situations sometimes produce high levels of anxiety, we might expect damaging effects. Beam (1955) showed that the stress of doctoral examinations and oral reports did produce decreased ability to learn nonsense syllables, but improved conditionability.

Since individuals obviously differ in their reactions to stress, a number of investigators have attempted to devise questionnaires which might differentiate individuals who respond differently in stress situations. In addition to the Taylor Manifest Anxiety Scale used in the studies cited above, a number of experimenters have used the Mandler-Sarason Test Anxiety Questionnaire. Individuals who score as highly anxious on this questionnaire responded with poorer performance after reports on their success or failure while those with low anxiety improved (Mandler and Sarason, 1952). The Interfering Tendency Questionnaire (which correlates well with the Taylor scale), developed by Waterhouse and Child (1953), also differentiates individuals responding differently to failure. Under neutral conditions individuals scoring high in interfering tendencies do better than low scorers but after failure the high scorers do worse; Williams (1955) confirmed this finding.

Since anxiety is generally believed to be increased by uncertainty, we would expect the anxious person to work most effectively in highly structured situations. This hypothesis is partially supported by the research of D. E. P. Smith, et al. (1956), who found that anxious students who were permeable (extroverted) made optimal progress in a remedial reading course when taught by directive methods. Impermeable anxious students, however, were unaffected by differences in teaching methods. H. C. Smith (1955), on the other hand, found that students high in achievement anxiety did not perform better in highly structured than in less-structured classes. In the psychology course studied, students preferred the classes with a high degree of structure; the more anxious students differentiated more clearly in their preference for sections with a high degree of structure.

The relationship between anxiety and performance on classroom examinations administered under varying conditions has been the subject of several experiments. To test experimentally whether the anxiety created by tests interfered with performance, half of the students in a University of Michigan experiment were given answer sheets with spaces for comments, and half were given standard sheets. Measures of students' feelings about the tests failed to show any difference between the two groups; but the students who had the opportunity to write comments made higher scores on the test (McKeachie, Pollie, and Speisman, 1955). The findings suggested that student anxiety during classroom examinations builds up to such a point that it interferes with memory and problem solving. Reducing the stress of the examination by permitting students to write comments thus resulted in improved performance.

This interpretation was supported in a study by Calvin, McGuigan, and Sullivan (1957), who found that students who were given a chance to write comments were superior to control students. Those for whom the opportunity was most important were the highly anxious students as measured by the Taylor Anxiety Scale. Similarly, Smith and Rockett (1958) found that instructions to write comments significantly interacted with anxiety—helping the performance of high-anxiety students but hurting the performance of students low in anxiety.

Carrier (1957) found that one of the most important variables in determining reaction to stressful examination conditions was sex. Women were much more detrimentally affected than men by stress situations. Need for achievement and need for affiliation failed to predict reactions to the stress situation. However, the permeable students, as measured by Smith's Sa-S scale, were detrimentally affected by stress.

In a succeeding experiment (McKeachie, 1958c) half of 350 students taking a test received conventional IBM answer sheets; half received answer sheets with space for comments. In addition, half of the students had received one of the tranquilizing drugs, meprobamate ("Milltown"), from a physician associated with the Mental Health Research Institute, while the other half received a placebo. If most students are too anxious, such a drug should improve test scores. The results did not confirm this hypothesis. Students having the Milltown reported experiencing less anxiety during the examination than did the placebo group, but they did not make better scores. The sex-drug interaction, however, was significant, with women benefiting from the drug more than men. Thus sex again turned out to be an important variable. The results make sense if we assume a curvilinear relationship between anxiety and performance, with women more anxious than men. In this case reduced anxiety for women resulted in improved performance, but reduced anxiety resulted in poorer performance for men.

Using oral rather than written responses, Hoehn and Saltz (1956) similarly found that anxious students were helped by interviews while rigid students were more likely to fail if interviewed. The results were further affected by the type of interview, with interviews in which students were encouraged to gripe producing the interaction noted above, while interviews oriented toward the student's goals and sources of satisfaction did not produce the effect.

The experimental results on interaction of anxiety and teaching variables are thus tantalizing enough to stimulate further work, but are not consistent enough to lead to any stable generalizations. It appears that the performance of many students is detrimentally affected by anxiety. Well-structured classes and opportunities to blow off steam may help such students.

The implications for adult education are not clear. Undoubtedly adult students differ greatly in anxiety, but we do not know whether the sex differences which loom large in college populations hold for adult classes. If Syracuse is typical (Knox, undated), the majority of adult students are men, and we would thus not expect stress to have such detrimental effects as for women students.

The Achievement Motive

The achievement motive has been the object of a great deal of research in the past 15 years. One would guess that people who choose to enroll in adult education courses would be higher in the achievement motive than the general population. Jenkins (in Miller, 1960) points out that the learning situation is likely to be perceived as an evaluation situation in which we are particularly sensitive about our own sense of worth. We would thus expect individuals with a strong fear of failure to avoid enrolling in adult classes. Moreover, Veroff, Atkinson, Feld, and Gurin (1960) found that the achievement motive tends to be higher among middle aged individuals than among older or younger people. Thus adult classes may contain a high proportion of individuals with strong positive achievement motives.

The effect of achievement motivation upon learning is likely to be a complex one. The studies of Patton, and of Koenig and McKeachie discussed earlier indicate that individuals with relatively strong achievement motives do well and like classes in which students have a good deal of independent responsibility. McKeachie (1961) studied the performance of students differing in the achievement motivation in the classes of 31 college teachers differing in their emphasis upon achievement standards and competition. Achievement cues and the achievement motive interacted in determining grades in psychology. Students who scored in the mid-third of the distribution of achievement motive scores did best in the sections presenting fewer achievement cues. This is not unreasonable if this is a group high in fear of failure as suggested by Brown (1953), McClelland and Liberman (1949), and McClelland, Atkinson, Clark, and Lowell (1953). One would theorize that as achievement cues are increased, such students perform less well because they adopt defensive avoidance behaviors such as daydreaming or leaving the examination early (as described by Atkinson and Litwin).

Unfortunately this relationship did not hold for the other two courses studied. Again there was significant interaction between achievement cues and n Achievement[4] in determining grades, but it was the high n Achievement students who did best in the low cue sections. In fact the group for whom the difference was greatest was the men in the top third of the n Achievement distribution. These students made a grade point average of 2.1 in the high cue sections as compared with 2.6 in the low cue sections (4 = A).

Sex differences emerged in a significant three-way interaction between achievement cues, sex, and n Achievement predicting grades in the psychology course. As expected, men high in n Achievement did poorly in sections low in achievement cues. Women high in n Achievement did relatively better in low cue than high cue sections. In the other two courses studied (mathematics and French) men generally did better in low achievement sections than in sections high in cues for achievement while for women the differences were slight.

Ratings of class value indicate that both men and women high in the achievement motive preferred classes with a low level of achievement cues; students scoring low in n Achievement rated the high cue sections as more valuable. Even with the deviant psychology course included, overall, the student with a high need for achievement did best in the sections with fewer achievement cues.

For the student with high intrinsic motivation, rewards for achievement may be internalized so that when he is placed in a situation where the task involves some competitive standard of achievement, he is motivated and receives satisfaction when his achievement approaches or reaches his level of aspiration. Other students, however, may be dependent upon extrinsic rewards for achievement. Grades, praise, or some other form of recognition may be necessary for them to be motivated. What happens to these two types of students in a situation in which the extrinsic rewards are emphasized? Both types of students continue to work, but for the intrinsically motivated student some of the zest is gone.

One of the allurements of this explanation is that it can handle the troublesome divergencies of the psychology course. Although this course did not differ from others in achievement cues, it was taught in a more permissive manner. Thus in psychology we might expect a greater oppor-

---

4. n Achievement is commonly used as an abbreviation for need for achievement or the achievement motive.

tunity than in other courses for intrinsic motivation to find satisfaction within the sections with many achievement cues.

Intriguing results came from the interactions of achievement motivation with the degree to which the instructor made the steps to a good grade clear by announcing tests in class and indicating when student comments were right or wrong. Students who were high in achievement motivation and low in anxiety received higher grades in sections low on this feedback dimension than in high sections. Women low in achievement motivation and low in anxiety did not like nor do well in sections low in feedback. Men low in achievement motivation and low in anxiety did well in sections high in feedback but rated the value of the course as low.

The performance of the high n Achievement, low anxiety student fits the conception that a student with positive internalized motives, will do best in a situation where intrinsic rather than extrinsic rewards are maximized. The low-low students on the other hand may be characterized as possessing weak intrinsic motives and hence requiring more extrinsic pushes and pulls.

For adult educators the value of this study may not lie in the complexities of the specific results but in the general notion that adult education classes are likely to attract many students who do best when they are not pushed by emphasis upon the extrinsic motives likely to be satisfied by learning. These students can assume responsibility for their own learning and will do better if given some freedom.

Authoritarianism

One of the most actively studied research variables of the past decade has been authoritarianism. This variable has also been studied in relationship to college learning. Watson (1956) studied the effect of permissive and restrictive teaching and testing methods upon students differing in authoritarianism and permeability. The methods with highest satisfaction resulted when the student was tested in an atmosphere appropriate for his needs, permissive for permeable, restrictive for impermeable. This finding is in line with the finding of Bendig and Hountras (1959) that authoritarian students prefer a high degree of departmental control of instruction and with the Hoehn and Saltz and Carrier results reported earlier.

By far the most extensive studies of personality characteristics related to college achievement are those of Stern, Stein, and Bloom (1956) and Pace and Stern (1958). As we saw earlier, students high on variable akin to authoritarianism were found to gain more when taught in a homogeneous group. The instructor who taught this section found that he had to resist pressures from the students for lectures. He secured good results by using many direct questions, encouraging student responses, and vigorously defending absurd positions which even authoritarian students would argue against. Kuhlen's research (1955) suggests that older adults are likely to have more rigid and authoritarian attitudes than young people. Stern's results thus may have considerable significance for teachers of adults.

The Affiliation Motive

The affiliation motive as measured by the TAT is presumed to involve "concern with establishing, maintaining or restoring a positive affective relationship with another person." McKeachie (1961) hypothesized that students differing in affiliation motivation would be affected differentially by the "warmth" or friendliness of the instructor. This hypothesis was supported by a significant interaction between teacher warmth and student affiliation motivation in determining grades for all students in introductory psychology, and for men in mathematics and psychology courses.

Other interactions add complexities to this relationship. For women, warmth produced higher grades; men, on the other hand did more poorly in high warmth sections. Folklore, and some research, supports the notion that interpersonal relationships are more important to women than men. Thus it makes good sense that women should be favorably affected by affiliative cues. It may be that general feminine sensitivity to affiliation cues tends to wash out the effects of individual differences in n Affiliation in women. Offering support for this speculation is the fact that even the women low in n Affiliation tended to prefer the classes with high affiliation cues.

Recent studies of public school teachers by Cogan (1958) and Ryans (1960) indicate that a dimension characterized by friendly, integrative, affiliative, nurturant behavior is important in public school teaching. Teachers high in this dimension produced more student self-initiated work than teachers low in the dimension. Solomon (1962) found a similar teaching characteristic to be liked by adult students but not to be related to learning or comprehension. Veroff, Atkinson, Feld, and Gurin (1960) report that the affiliation motive tends to increase with age for men so that warmth and friendliness may be particularly important in classes for older adults.

Need for Power

Veroff (1957), who developed the scoring system for power motivation, describes the power motive as that "disposition directing behavior toward satisfactions contingent upon the control of the means of influencing another person." He found that students who scored high in power motivation enjoyed leadership and recognition and were rated by instructors as high in argumentativeness and in frequency of trying to convince others of their point of view in the classroom. McKeachie (1961) found that men high in power motivation received higher grades in classes in which student volunteering was prevalent than in classes in which student volunteering was uncommon. The converse was true for males low in power motivation. While we do not know whether or not adult classes have a selective effect in attracting individuals high in power motive, Gurin, Veroff, and Feld found this motive to be particularly high among men aged 21-34.

Conclusion

In summing up the studies on the interaction of personality characteristics and teaching methods as affecting student learning, it is safe to say that no major breakthrough has occurred, but that the results so far appear promising. Fortunately, multivariate statistical techniques now permit analysis of the complexities involved.

The most clear-cut results suggest that students of high intelligence profit most in developing critical thinking skills from classes taught by methods which permit a high degree of student participation. Anxious students perform better on examinations when the stress is reduced by giving them an opportunity to write comments or gripe. Students high in the achievement motive and independence do well in learning situations in which they have responsibility for their own learning. But independent study does not appear to strengthen independence.

It is clear that we need a good deal more research on adult classes before we can safely generalize from studies on college classes. Nevertheless one can make guesses on the basis of college results and on the assumption that adult students are higher in authoritarianism, rigidity, achievement motivation, affiliation motivation, and power motivation. From the studies of the three motives and from Beach's study of sociability one would guess that for both attitudinal and higher cognitive outcomes a friendly permissive teaching style would be most effective for adults. However, this must be balanced against the greater authoritarianism and rigidity of older students which would suggest that abrupt shifts to new teaching methods would be difficult for the students to accept and adjust to. It thus appears, as in most teaching situations, that the teacher cannot follow any general rule of thumb but must adjust his approach as he sizes up each class, and receives feedback from them.

One would suppose that classroom instruction is of much more importance in the success of an adult course than in a college course. For the adult, class is a special part of his activities offering a significant change from the problems of daily life; for the full time student, class periods follow one upon another in what all too often is a dreary, monotonous cycle. But for the college student, libraries, dormitory quiet hours, and even study dates gently impel him to study outside of class. For the adult, study time must be found in the midst of the competing demands of his family, job, and recreation activities.

This means that the college teacher with an extra evening extension class may not sufficiently differentiate his approaches to the different types of teaching. As Whipple (1957) points out, there is no one best method of teaching adults which can be used inflexibly. Rather the results of research can sensitize the teacher to aspects of the teaching situation of which he may formerly have been only vaguely aware. With this new awareness he will be better able to make use of his own and his students' resources.

References

Anderson, R. C. Learning in discussion: a resume of the authoritarian-democratic studies. Harvard educ. Rev., 1959, 29, 201-15.

Anderson, R. P., and Kell, B. L. Student attitudes about participation in classroom groups. J. educ. Res., 1954, 48, 255-67.

Ashmus, Mable, and Haigh, G. Some factors which may be associated with student choice between directive and non-directive classes.

Atkinson, J. W. (ed.). Motives in Fantasy, Action, and Society. Princeton: Van Nostrand, 1958.

Atkinson, J. W., and Litwin, G. H. An experimental study of need-achievement and examination anxiety. J. abnorm. soc. Psychol., 1960, 60, 52-63.

Beach, L. R. Sociability and academic achievement in various types of learning situations. J. educ. Psychol., 1960, 51, 208-12.

Beam, J. C. Serial learning and conditioning under real-life stress. J. abnorm. soc. Psychol., 1955, 51, 543-51.

Bendig, A. W. Ability and personality characteristics of introductory psychology instructors rated competent and empathic by their students. J. educ. Res., 1955, 48, 705-9.

Bendig, A. W., and Hountras, P. T. Anxiety, authoritarianism, and student attitude toward departmental control of college instruction. J. educ. Psychol., 1959, 50, 1-8.

Bills, R. E. Investigation of student centered teaching. J. educ. Res., 1952, 46, 313-19.

Brown, R. W. A derminant of the relationship between rigidity and authoritarianism. J. abnorm. soc. Psychol., 1953, 48, 469-76.

Burtt, H. E., Chassel, L. M., and Hatch, E. M. Efficiency of instruction in unselected and selected sections of elementary psychology. J. educ. Psychol., 1923, 14, 154-61.

Calvin, A. D., Hoffman, F. K., and Harden, E. L. The effect of intelligence and social atmosphere on group problem solving behavior. J. soc. Psychol., 1957, 45, 61-74.

Calvin, A. D., McGuigan, F. J., and Sullivan, M. W. A further investigation of the relationship between anxiety and classroom examination performance. J. educ. Psychol., 1957, 48, 240-44.

Carrier, N. A. The relationship of certain personality measures to examination performance under stress. J. educ. Psychol., 1957, 48, 510-20.

Churchill, Ruth, and Baskin, S. Experiment on independent study. Yellow Springs, O., Antioch Coll., 1958. (Mimeograph)

Cogan, M. L. The behavior of teachers and the productive behavior of their pupils: II Trait analysis. J. exper. Educ., 1958, 27, 107-24.

Cross, D. An investigation of the relationships between students' expressions of satisfaction with certain aspects of the college classroom situation and their achievement on final examinations. (Unpublished honors thesis, Univ. of Mich., 1958.)

Deignan, F. J. A comparison of the effectiveness of two group discussion methods. (Unpublished doctoral dissertation, Boston Univ., 1955 [Diss. Abstr., 1956, 16, 1110-1111].)

Della-Piana, G. M. Searching orientation and concept learning. J. educ. Psychol., 1957, 48, 245-53.

Elliott, P. N. Characteristics and relationships of various criteria of college and university teaching. Purdue Univ. Studies in Higher Educ., 1950, 70, 5-61.

Goldstein, A. A controlled comparison of the project method with standard laboratory teaching in pharmacology. J. med. Educ., 1956, 31, 365-75.

Gruber, N. E., and Weitman, M. Self-directed Study. Boulder, Colo.: Univ. of Colorado, Beh. Res. Lab. Report 19, 1962.

Guetzkow, H., Kelly, E. L., and McKeachie, W. J. An experimental comparison of recitation, discussion, and tutorial methods in college teaching. J. educ. Psychol., 1954, 45, 193-209.

Havighurst, R. J., and Orr, Betty. Adult education and adult needs. Chicago: Center for the Study of Liberal Education for Adults, 1956.

Haythorn, W., Couch, A., Haefner, D., Langham, P., and Carter, L. The effects of varying combinations of authoritarian and equalitarian leader followers. J. abnorm. soc. Psychol., 1956, 53, 210-19.

Hoffman, L. R. Homogeneity of member personality and its effect on group problem solving. J. abnorm. soc. Psychol., 1959, 58, 27-32.

Hudelson, E. Class Size at the College Level. Minneapolis: Univ. of Minn. Press, 1928.

Jenkins, R. L. The relative effectiveness of two methods of teaching written and spoken English. (Unpublished doctoral dissertation, Mich. State, 1952 [Diss. Abstr.] 1952, 12, 268.)

Johnson, D. M., and Smith, H. C. Democratic leadership in the college classroom. Psychol. Monogr., 1953, 56, No. 11 (Whole No. 361).

Katona, G. Organizing and Memorizing. New York: Columbia Univ. Press, 1940.

Katz, D. Gestalt Psychology. New York: Ronald Press, 1950.

Kersh, B. Y. The adequacy of "meaning" as an explanation for the superiority of learning by independent discovery. J. educ. Psychol., 1959, 49, 282-92.

Knox, A. B. A summary report on adult college students. Univ. College, Syracuse Univ. (Undated).

Koenig, Kathryn, and McKeachie, W. J. Personality and independent study. J. educ. Psychol., 1959, 50, 132-34.

Krumboltz, J. D., and Farquar, W. W. The effect of three teaching methods on achievement and motivational outcomes in a how-to-study course. Psychol. Monogr., 1957, 71, No. 14 (Whole No. 443).

Kuhlen, R. G. Aging and life adjustment. In Birren, J. E. (ed.), Handbook of Aging and the Individual., Chicago: Univ. of Chicago Press, 1959.

Kuhlen, R. G. Patterns of adult development. In Murphy, G., and Kuhlen, R., Psychological Needs of Adults, Chicago: Center for the Study of Liberal Education for Adults, 1955.

Lahti, A. M. The inductive-deductive method and the physical science laboratory. J. exp. Educ., 1956, 24, 149-63.

Landsman, T. An experimental study of a student-centered learning method. (Unpublished doctoral dissertation, Syracuse Univ., 1950.)

Longstaff, H. P. Analysis of some factors conditioning learning in general psychology. J. appl. Psychol., 1932, 16, 948, 131-66.

McClelland, D. C., Atkinson, J. W., Clark, R. A., and Lowell, E. L. The Achievement Motive. New York: Appleton-Century-Crafts, 1953.

McClelland, D. C., and Liberman, A. M. The effect of need for achievement on recognition of need-related words. J. Pers., 1949, 18, 236-51.

McCullough, Celeste, and VanAtta, E. L. Experimental evaluation of teaching programs utilizing a block of independent work. Paper read at Symposium; Experimental studies in learning independently. Amer. Psychol. Assoc., Washington, D.C., Sept., 1958.

McGeoch, J. A., and Irion, A. L. The psychology of human learning. New York: Longmans, 1952, 46 ff.

McKeachie, W. J. Students, groups, and teaching methods. Amer. Psychologist., 1958, 13, 580-84.

McKeachie, W. J. Appraising teaching effectiveness. In W. J. McKeachie (Ed.), The appraisal of teaching in large universities, Ann Arbor, Mich.: Univ. of Mich., 1959, 32-36.

McKeachie, W. J. Motivation, teaching methods and college learning. In Jones, M. R., Nebraska Symposium on Motivation 1961, Lincoln, Neb.: Univ. of Neb. Press, 1961, 111-42.

McKeachie, W. J., Lin, Y. G., Forrin, B., and Teevan, R. Individualized teaching in elementary psychology. J. educ. Psychol., 1960, 51, 285-91.

McKeachie, W. J., Pollie, D., and Speisman, J. Relieving anxiety in classroom examinations. J. abnorm. soc. Psychol., 1955, 50, 93-98.

Macomber, F. G., and Siegel, L. Experimental study in instructional procedures. Progress Report No. 1, Oxford, Ohio: Miami Univ., 1956.

Macomber, F. G., and Siegel, L. A study of large group teaching procedures. Educ. Res., 1957a, 220-29.

Macomber, F. G., and Siegel, L. Experimental study in instructional procedures. Progress Report No. 2, Oxford, Ohio: Miami Univ., 1957b.

Mandler, G., and Sarason, S. B. A study of anxiety and learning. J. abnorm. soc. Psychol., 1952, 47, 166-73.

Miller, Marilyn V. (Ed.). On Teaching Adults: An Anthology. Chicago: Center for the Study of Liberal Education for Adults, 1960.

Novak, J. D. An experimental comparison of a conventional and a project centered method of teaching a college general botany course. J. exp. Educ., 1958, 26, 217-30.

Pace, R. C., and Stern, G. C. A criterion study of college environment. Syracuse Univ.: Psychol. Res. Center, 1958.

Parsons, T. S. A comparison of instruction by kinescope, correspondence study, and customary classroom procedures. J. educ. Psychol., 1957, 48, 27-40.

Parsons, T. S., Ketcham, W. A., and Beach, L. R. Effects of varying degrees of student interaction and student-teacher contact in college courses. Paper read at Amer. Social. Soc., Seattle, Washington, August, 1958.

Parsons, T. S., Ketcham, W. A., and Beach, L. R. Students, teachers and fellow students: a study of instructional interactions and outcomes (Dittoed) 11 pp.

Patton, J. A. A study of the effects of student acceptance of responsibility and motivation on course behavior. (Unpublished doctoral dissertation, Univ. of Mich., 1955.)

Rasmussen, G. R. Evaluation of a student-centered and instructor-centered method of conducting a graduate course in education. J. educ. Psychol., 1956, 47, 449-61.

Remmers, H. H. Learning, effort, and attitude as affected by three methods of instruction in elementary psychology. Purdue Univ. Stud. higher Educ., 1933, 21.

Ryans, D. G. Characteristics of Teachers. Washington: Amer. Council on Educ., 1960.

Sarason, I. Empirical findings and theoretical problems in the use of anxiety scales. Psychol. Bull., 1960, 57, 403-15.

Scheideman, Norma V. An experiment in teaching psychology. J. appl. Psychol., 1929, 13, 188-91.

Seashore, C. E. Elementary psychology. An outline of a course by the project method. Aims and Progress of Res., No. 153. Iowa City, Iowa: Univ. of Iowa, 1928.

Seibert, W. F. An evaluation of televised instruction in college English composition. Purdue Univ.: TVRP Report No. 5, 1958.

Slomowitz, M. A comparison of personality changes and content achievement gains occurring in two modes of instruction. (Unpublished doctoral dissertation, New York Univ., 1955 [Diss. Abstr., 1955, 15, 1790].)

Smith, D. E. P., Wood, R. L., Downer, J. W., and Raygor, A. L. Reading improvement as a function of student personality and teaching methods. J. educ. Psychol., 1956, 47, 47-58.

Smith, H. C. Team work in the college class. J. educ. Psychol., 1955, 46, 274-86.

Smith, W. F., and Rockett, F. C. Test performance as a function of anxiety, instructor, and instructions. J. educ. Res., 1958, 52, 138-41.

Solomon, D. Teaching styles and student achievement. Paper read at AERA meeting, Feb. 20, 1962, Atlantic City, N.J.

Spence, K. W., and Taylor, Janet A. Anxiety and strength of the USC as determiners of the amount of eyelid conditioning. J. exp. Psychol., 1951, 42, 183-88.

Stern, G. G. Environments for learning. In Sanford, R. N., The American College, New York: Wiley, 1962.

Stern, G. G., Stein, M. I., and Bloom, B. S. Methods in Personality Assessment. Glencoe, Ill.: Free Press, 1956.

Sturgis, H. W. The relationship of the teacher's knowledge of the student's background to the effectiveness of teaching. A study of the extent to which the effectiveness of teaching is related to the teacher's knowledge of the student's personal background. (Unpublished doctoral dissertation, New York Univ., 1958 [Diss. Abstr., 1959, 19, No. 11].)

Tharp, J. B. Sectioning in romance language classes at the University of Illinois. In Studies in Modern Language Teaching, New York: Macmillan, 1930, 367-432.

Thistlethwaite, D. L. College environments and the development of talent. Science, 1959, 130, 71-76.

Thistlethwaite, D. L. College press and changes in study plans of talented students. Evanston, Ill.: Natl. Merit Scholarship Corp., 1960.

Timmel, G. B. A study of the relationship between method of teaching a college course in mental hygiene and change in student adjustment status. (Unpublished doctoral dissertation, Cornell University, 1954 [Diss. Abstr., 1955, 15, 90].)

Ullrich, O. A. An experimental study in ability grouping. (Unpublished doctoral dissertation, Univ. of Texas, 1926.)

Veroff, J. Development and validation of a projective measure of power motivation. J. abnorm. soc. Psychol., 1957, 54, 1-8.

Veroff, J., Atkinson, J. W., Feld, S. C., and Gurin, G. The use of thematic apperception to assess motivation in a nationwide interview study. <u>Psychol. Monogr.</u>, 1960, <u>74</u>, No. 12 (Whole No. 499).

Ward, J. Group-study vs. lecture-demonstration method in physical science instruction for general education college students. <u>J. exp. Educ.</u>, 1956, <u>24</u>, 197-210.

Waterhouse, I. K., and Child, I. L. Frustration and the quality of performance. <u>J. Pers.</u>, 1953, <u>21</u>, 298-311.

Watson, R. P. The relationship between selected personality variables, satisfaction, and academic achievement in defined classroom atmospheres. (Unpublished doctoral dissertation, Univ. of Mich., 1956.)

Whipple, J. B. <u>Especially for Adults</u>. Chicago: Center for the Study of Liberal Education for Adults, 1957.

Williams, J. E. Mode of failure, interference tendencies, and achievement imagery. <u>J. abnorm. soc. Psychol.</u>, 1955, <u>51</u>, 573-80.

Wispe, L. G. Evaluating section teaching methods in the introductory course. <u>J. educ. Res.</u>, 1951, <u>45</u>, 161-86.

Wolfle, D. The relative efficiency of constant and varied stimulation during learning. <u>J. comp. Psychol.</u>, 1935, <u>19</u>, 5-27.

Zander, A. Student motives and teaching methods in four informal adult classes. <u>Adult Educ.</u>, 1951, <u>2</u>, 27-31.

ROSTER OF PARTICIPANTS

Speakers and Discussants

David P. Ausubel, Professor of Educational Psychology, University of Illinois

James E. Birren, Chief, Section on Aging, National Institute of Mental Health

Earnest Brandenburg, Dean of University College, Washington University (St. Louis)

Bettye M. Caldwell, Lecturer in Psychology, Syracuse University

Richard T. Deters, S.J., Dean of Evening College, Xavier University (Cincinnati)

Robert Kleemeier, Professor of Psychology, Washington University (St. Louis)

Raymond G. Kuhlen, Professor of Psychology, Syracuse University

Wilbert J. McKeachie, Professor of Psychology, University of Michigan

Harry L. Miller, Associate Professor of Education, Hunter College

Bernice L. Neugarten, Associate Professor, Committee on Human Development, University of Chicago

William A. Owens, Professor of Psychology, Purdue University

Paul H. Sheats, Dean of University Extension, University of California (Los Angeles)